Migrating ServiceNow® Event Management

Insights and recommendations on how to move from your existing event management system to ServiceNow ITOM

Frank Tate

DEDICATION

I dedicate this book to my wife, Kelly, who has been a silent but extremely helpful member of every implementation team I've been on for the past 11 years. I could talk about her industrial engineering degree or her MBA or the fact that she's a lot smarter than me, but she's too modest to allow me to do that.

TABLE OF CONTENTS

1 Introduction

This book is aimed primarily at IT professionals who will be migrating an existing event management system to ServiceNow® ITOM. Your company has some kind of monitoring and event management systems in place, along with a ticketing system like BMC Remedy or CA Service Desk, and you now need to implement ServiceNow ITOM. The goal of this book is to provide a high-level perspective of the often-hidden tasks that need to be performed as part of a successful implementation along with some useful technical details and lessons learned. The ServiceNow product documentation is terrific and provides an amazing level of detail regarding customizing and using the product, but I have found that it does not address some of the organizational and environmental challenges that are involved in migrating to ServiceNow ITOM. My reason for writing this book is to provide some of that missing information.

This book is also meant to provide background information on many of the aspects involved with monitoring and event management in general. This background information is useful to anyone unfamiliar with these topics and who is working on a ServiceNow ITOM engagement.

This book will address how to identify your current state of monitoring and event management, and then will present details you need to consider when attempting to architect a solution in ServiceNow. We will discuss some of the problems you will likely encounter and many of the incorrect assumptions that can steer you in the wrong direction.

Your company has most likely been doing some type of event management before now, possibly without a lot of enterprise oversight. Implementing ServiceNow ITOM will allow you to change that. Even if you are embracing DevOps, your company's IT systems need to be monitored and governed centrally to some degree to allow them to operate as efficiently as possible. Sending alarms to a centralized system will definitely cause some headaches, but that pain is necessary to let all affected stakeholders know exactly what's going on in the environment. No one likes a bright light shining on their local problems, but this light will allow the event management processes to grow stronger and will allow the enterprise to run better, without relying on the individual expertise of one or two people.

Most of the stories you read about IT are about the **new shiny thing** that "everyone" is doing. The truth of the matter is that implementing new technology in a greenfield environment is typically easy because there are no legacy concerns to deal with. It is terrific if you are deploying everything to a hybrid cloud using an orchestration product that was written for that very task, and you're tagging all of your resources so they can easily be identified in any context. The hard part is dealing with the legacy environment that is in place now, replicating similar functions in a new system, no matter how backward that behavior appears to be. The existing behavior is what is keeping your infrastructure up and running today. You cannot simply turn it off. You can, however, migrate to or incorporate new tools that offer you the flexibility to implement more advanced operational efficiencies. And that is where this book comes in handy.

This book does not cover much user interface customization. I believe that area of the product is covered sufficiently in the product documentation, community forums, videos, and other books. This book covers the groundwork and backend configuration that is not found elsewhere.

2   First things first: This is Going to be Painful.

There is no sugar-coating it. Migrating to ServiceNow ITOM is going to be very painful, through no fault of the software. If it is easy at first, just know that something will come up eventually that will require more work than anyone estimated. ServiceNow ITOM is a completely new-to-you system, which is changing the way your company is running IT, and that necessarily means that there will be large changes. If no changes were needed, why would your company have signed a multi-million-dollar deal to implement ServiceNow?

The purchase of ServiceNow is often the start of the real "digital transformation" for any organization. There are lots of different definitions of "digital transformation" because it means different things to different people, and that is OK. From an IT perspective, my broad definition of "digital transformation" is:

> Moving toward a tightly integrated, highly automated enterprise, where all manual inputs and interventions are constantly reviewed with the purpose of automating them.

If you want to see an example of a digitally transformed environment, look no further than AWS (Amazon Web Services, aka Amazon Cloud). If you have not looked deep into AWS or one of the other large cloud providers, do that NOW; acloudguru.com is a terrific resource for all kinds of cloud-related information. AWS was purpose-built to provide observable, scalable, repeatable IT infrastructure and supporting services to any number of customers. As their IT department encounters challenges or receives requests for new services, they review those to determine how solutions to those requests can be generalized and made available to the rest of their user base. To me, there is simply no better example of digital transformation than AWS itself.

This book will provide you with information about ServiceNow ITOM to hopefully help you make that part of the implementation easier. You do still need to recognize that there are lots of other components of ServiceNow that your organization may be implementing, and you need to constantly learn as much as you can to help the overall implementation go as smoothly as possible.

The first rule of a smooth transition is to document exactly what the process looks like now so that it can be compared with the behavior in ServiceNow. This is covered in detail in Section 2 of this book, but it is definitely worth mentioning now. The single most destructive behavior I have seen when migrating to ServiceNow is to force users into the new system with no regard for how they performed their jobs in the old system. It is crucially important to understand the current system and processes so that you can explain any changes that are being made, and so you can explain those changes in the context of the legacy process.

The second rule of any enterprise software implementation is to ensure that you create "consumable and understandable" deliverables. The exact definition of "consumable and understandable" varies based on the receiver of the information, so you need to constantly evaluate your target audience to determine if your deliverables are appropriate in your situation. In many cases you will need to produce different versions of the same deliverable so that the ideas and information presented can be adequately understood by your audience. As an IT consultant, the production of consumable and understandable deliverables is probably my highest daily priority.

Section A: Background Information

This section provides background information on monitoring and event management in general. It is critically important to understand that these topics are both extremely complex. I have found that these topics are often described at a very high level that obscures the challenges that are involved in the technical details of each. This section provides a number of these frequently overlooked details.

The chapters included in this section are:

3. What is monitoring?

4. Event Management

3 What is monitoring?

This section is a primer on monitoring. If you are already familiar with this topic, move on to the next section.

Monitoring your IT infrastructure takes many forms. The simplest type of monitoring is an agent or service that records some number of metrics (e.g., disk space used) every cycle (where a cycle is some time period). This data is collected into a time series database, where it is leveraged for real-time dashboards and historical reports.

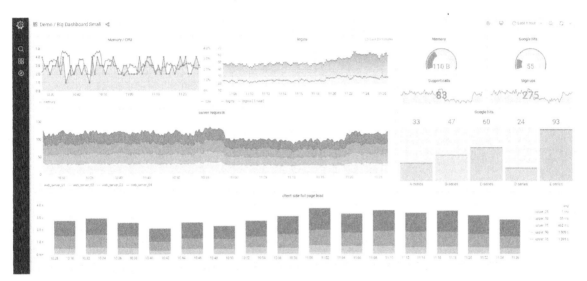

Figure 3-1 Grafana dashboard

Exactly what data is shown on a dashboard or report depends on the consumers of the dashboard or report. Dashboard and report creation are topics that are beyond the scope of this book, but we will discuss some important aspects throughout the text. One example of this type of monitoring is Prometheus, DataDog and Amazon CloudWatch (though all of these have much more advanced capabilities).

Most of these monitoring tools also include some type of alert facility, where you can specify that some action is performed when a defined threshold is reached. Most often, the action that is taken for a breached threshold is that some type of message is generated. Precisely what types of message can be sent depend entirely on the monitoring system you are using. Newer monitoring systems generally have the ability to make an outgoing REST API call, but many older systems are limited to only sending SNMP traps or a message in a proprietary format.

Another type of monitoring tool is a log file monitor, which looks for some pattern in a log file, and takes an action when that pattern is found. Splunk is currently one of the most popular log file aggregation and monitoring tools. Splunk allows you to send all your log file messages to a central repository, when rules can be centrally created to specify which actions will be taken based on different criteria. Again, a common action is to send a message "somewhere".

Yet another type of monitoring utilizes a "robot" of some type to regularly test an application (e.g., a web application) and generate a message if the application doesn't behave exactly as expected. Dynatrace, AppDynamics and IBM Application Performance Management are examples of this type of monitoring.

The most integrated type of monitoring is one where the application itself is instrumented with function calls to record performance and success/failure results to a central system. Dynatrace, AppDynamics, New Relic and IBM all have offerings in this space. These function calls either write data to a log file (to be picked up by a log file monitor) and/or send messages to some central system. Again, the central system is configured with some number of rules that say, essentially, "when X happens, take action Y", and "action Y" is usually sending a message "somewhere".

And this is where Event Management comes into play. Many companies define one or more actions to send an email to the appropriate people and/or to create a ticket when a threshold is crossed. Integrating your monitoring system(s) with ServiceNow will involve sending a message to ServiceNow. That message will create a ServiceNow **Event**, **Alert**, or **Incident**. Later in the book we will discuss the different integration options that are available.

Note: Prior to the Paris release, ServiceNow ITOM did not have any monitoring capabilities itself. With the Paris release, ServiceNow offers the Agent Client Collector on Linux and Windows to perform monitoring in your environment. This agent is built on the Sensu framework. More details can be found at sensu.io.

Throughout this book, you will see terms like "as appropriate" and "as needed", which may be frustrating at first. Hopefully, by the end of the book you will realize that this ambiguity is necessary because all of the behavior you define is completely dependent upon the goals defined by the stakeholders in your organization.

3.1   Monitoring Complex Applications and Environments
If you are not already familiar with multi-tiered applications, virtual machines, containers, Kubernetes, and service mesh (to name just a few), you should invest some time researching

these technologies. All of these are almost certainly in use in your environment, and you need to understand the architecture of each so that you understand what is being monitored.

As an example, here is a sample architecture of a cloud-native AWS application.

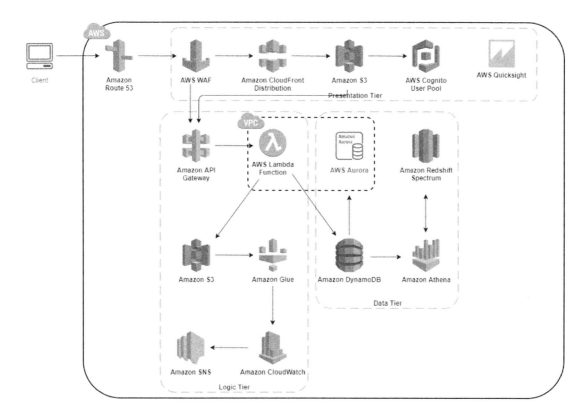

Figure 3-2 Sample AWS Application Architecture

This diagram is relatively straightforward. As a matter of fact, all of the components can be monitored to some degree using the same tool because everything is a service within the same public cloud. In the world of legacy applications, however, the applications have the same amount of complexity, but they contain all kinds of different applications, components, and services from different vendors, each with a different type of monitoring available. Basically, this picture is nice, but in the world of legacy applications, often no such diagram exists. Furthermore, some or most of the components are not even monitored. I am presenting this information to illuminate the point that a legacy environment is extremely messy, and there is no one straightforward way to monitor it.

Another complication with legacy environments is that there are multiple different support teams responsible for different components, some of which may be running on a single system. For example, the Operating Systems Team may be responsible for some parts of a server, but the Database Administration team is responsible for the database-related resources and the Application Infrastructure team is responsible for the application server-related resources. Another possibility is that you have multiple different Application Teams responsible for different applications on the same host. This is the case with WebSphere- or WebLogic-based applications, for example.

4   Event Management

According to Wikipedia, ITIL defines Event Management as "the process that monitors all events that occur through the IT Infrastructure. It allows for normal operation and also detects and escalates exception conditions". Wikipedia defines an Event as "any detectable or discernible occurrence that has significance for the management of the IT Infrastructure or the delivery of IT service and evaluation of the impact a deviation might cause to the services. Events are typically notifications created by an IT service, Configuration Item (CI) or monitoring tool".

To have event management, you need to be monitoring "something" and sending out some kind of message when some condition exists, or some threshold is exceeded. An event management system provides you with the ability to capture these messages in a centralized system so that they can be **normalized**, **enriched**, **correlated**, and **displayed in a meaningful context**.

I will break down that last sentence by describing the different actions described:

> **normalized:** Each ServiceNow Event is a row in the **em_event** table, which means that each event is a group of name/value pairs, where the possible names are pre-defined. Some of those column or attribute names are **message_key**, **metric_name**, **node**, **resource**, **type**, **severity**, and **additional_info**, to name a few of the most important ones. Normalization is the process of converting every message into a common format with all of the required fields.

> **enriched:** Events often do not contain all pertinent pieces of information. As an example, consider a disk space monitor running on a server. When that monitor fires because the disk is almost full, the event will contain the hostname, the name of the disk, and the percent of free space. What it does not contain is geographic information such as where the particular server is located, or the administrative contact for that server. The ServiceNow CMDB (Configuration Management Database) can be leveraged to provide this enriched data, but it is almost never contained in the event itself.

> **correlated:** One goal of event management is to decrease the number of duplicate alerts in the environment. Consider the case of a disk that is almost full. The monitor for that disk may send a message every 15 seconds. If all those messages have to be individually addressed by an operator, it can quickly become a time-consuming process. All these duplicate (or essentially duplicate) messages should be grouped together in some way that only alerts an operator once for this

particular problem. This is an example of correlating events. ServiceNow correlates events in several ways, but the most basic way is in the creation of an Alert. Every actionable event will have an Alert created for it, and identical (or close-to-identical) events will all be associated with the same Alert.

displayed in a meaningful context: An event management system should allow you to see events in relation to the systems and business services or applications which they impact. This allows an engineer to visually perform an impact analysis of each event.

The following is a flowchart of ITIL Event Management from AXELOS.

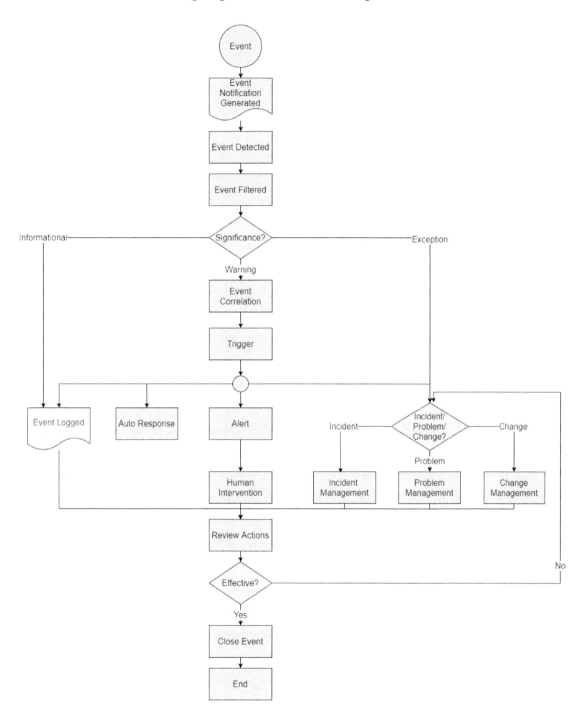

Figure 4-1 Event Management in ITIL

As you read through this book, you will realize that this diagram is missing a lot of details that are critical to successful event management. ITIL is a process framework, but it is neither prescriptive nor detailed in my opinion. Each organization working to implement ITIL (or any other framework) is responsible for defining the gory details. This book will provide you with the tools required to do some amount of that work.

4.1   Event Management Scenario

If you do not have an official event management system in place, here's an example of something that's likely happening today in your environment:

> A database has an issue that is written to the Windows Error Log. You are using MS SCCM for monitoring your Windows servers. SCCM sends an email to a Windows database administrator with the error message. The database administrator restarts the database, and the error no longer exists.

The above example appears to show that the problem was quickly resolved without the need to notify anyone else in the organization. In reality, however, that database is used by multiple customer-facing applications, all of which experienced outages when the database was restarted, resulting in the loss of real revenue and employee productivity. A centralized event management system can show the database issue in the context of all of the dependent applications, allowing an administrator to perform a full impact analysis before taking any drastic action. A centralized system management system also can capture downtime to use in Service Level Agreement (SLA) calculations and provides you with the ability to run reports regularly to view the stability of the environment. All these things are missed (or are provided in different ways across multiple different systems) if you do not have a centralized event management system in place.

4.2   What is an Event?

Basically, an Event in ServiceNow is a group of name/value pairs. The easiest way to view an event in my opinion is to view it as JSON data. The following is the JSON representation of a Linux filesystem event that contains enough data to identify the affected CI.

```
{
    "description": "/var filesystem on host ftserver1 is 99% full",
    "event_class": "FT ITM PROD",
    "metric_name": "ITM_Linux_Logical_Disk_Crit",
    "node": "ftserver1",
```

```
    "resolution_state": "New",
    "resource": "/var",
    "severity": "4",
    "source": "IBM Tivoli Monitoring",
    "type": "logical disk",
    "ci_type": "cmdb_ci_file_system",
    "message_key": "FT ITM PROD:ftserver1:ITM_Linux_Logical_Disk_Crit:/var",
    "additional_info": "{
            \"ft_situation_name\": \"ITM_Linux_Logical_Disk_Crit\",
            \"ft_tems\": \"HUBTEMS\",
            \"ft_sourceip\": \"10.10.10.20\",
            \"ft_bsmid\": \"ftserver1_897\",
            \"mount_point\": \"/var\"
    }"
}
```

A description of the event data follows.

First, JSON data is always inside curly braces, and inside the braces, the format is **"name":"value"**. Each **"name"** is the name of a column in the **em_event** table (e.g., **description, event_class,** etc.). So, on to descriptions of each of the fields:

"**description**": "/var filesystem on host ftserver1 is 99% full",
The **description** field should contain a user-readable description of the event. In this case, we can see that this event was generated because a filesystem is almost completely full.

"**event_class**": "FT ITM PROD",
The label displayed in the UI for this field is "Source Instance". So the value of the **event_class** field should uniquely identify the overall system that caused the event to be created. In this case, this event was created by my (FT) IBM Tivoli Monitoring (ITM) Production (PROD) environment.

"**metric_name**": "ITM_Linux_Logical_Disk_Critical",
The **metric_name** value is used to describe the type or kind of event. This particular event was created by the monitor named "ITM_Linux_Logical_Disk_Critical". In general, all events with this same value for **metric_name** should be so similar that you should be able to process all of them

with a single Event Rule. There are exceptions to every rule, but in general you should plan to have at least one Event Rule for each different value of **metric_name** in your environment.

   "**node**": "ftserver1",
The value in the **node** field is used to find the server, host or device impacted by this particular event. In this case, the hostname of the impacted device is a server with a hostname of "ftserver1". There should be some kind of CI (the class of which is derived from the cmdb_ci_hardware class) with this same name.

   "**resolution_state**": "New",
Events that represent a problem should always have a value of "New" in the **resolution_state** field. Events that indicate that a problem no longer exists (aka "clearing events") should have a value of "Closing" in this field.

   "**resource**": "/var",
In general, it is recommended that **type** should be used to specify the type of impacted resource, and **resource** should specify the name of the resource. This is not a strict rule, and you may find that you want to use these fields for some other purpose.

   "**severity**": "4",
severity specifies the severity of the condition that caused the event to be generated. Your organization will need to define what each severity (values 0-6 by default) means as it relates to events and alerts.

   "**source**": "IBM Tivoli Monitoring",
source is often the top-level filter applied when searching for Events and Alerts. This should specify the type of system that generated this particular event. Here the value is "IBM Tivoli Monitoring". Notice that **event_class** contains a related, but more specific value. In the environment that generated this event, I have multiple IBM Tivoli Monitoring environments: DEV, QA and PROD. **source** specifies the type of system (IBM Tivoli Monitoring) and **event_class** specifies the specific environment of that type that generated the event (FT ITM PROD).

   "**type**": "logical disk",

In general, it is recommended that **type** should be used to specify the type of impacted resource, and **resource** should specify the name of the resource. This is not a strict rule, and you may find that you want to use these fields for some other purpose.

 "**ci_type**": "cmdb_ci_file_system",
ci_type is optional when creating an event, but it is extremely useful. This column is used to specify the type or class of the impacted CI. This tells the CI binding process that the impacted CI is an instance of this class.

 "**message_key**": "FT ITM PROD:ftserver1:ITM_Linux_Logical_Disk_Crit:/var",
message_key is a column in both the **em_event** and **em_alert** tables. It is important because this is the primary field used to coalesce multiple events into a single alert. Specifically, any two events that have the same value for **message_key** will be associated with the *same* alert. This is an extremely important characteristic of ServiceNow Event Management.

 "**additional_info**": "{
        \"ft_situation_name\": \"ITM_Linux_Logical_Disk_Crit\",
        \"ft_tems\": \"HUBTEMS\",
        \"ft_sourceip\": \"10.10.10.20\",
        \"ft_bsmid\": \"ftserver1_897\",
        \"mount_point\": \"/var\"
 }"
additional_info is a uniquely customizable column in the **em_event** table. The value of this field is a string containing JSON data itself. Notice that the value is enclosed in double-quotes because it's a string, and then the value starts with an open brace and ends with a closing brace, with name/value pairs inside. The double-quotes inside the braces are escaped because they are actually part of the data. You can provide almost any name/value pairs that you want in this field. This allows you to send any and all relevant information in each event, without having to modify the **em_event** table. In this field you can see multiple names that begin with "ft_". I do this to ensure that the names don't conflict with any in the system. Now notice that I am providing the name "mount_point" with a value of "/var". This name/value pair will be used by the CI binding process to bind to the CI that:

1. Is contained by the CI referenced in the node field and

2. Is an instance of class "cmdb_ci_file_system" that has the value "/var" in its **mount_point** field.

This will be discussed in more detail later.

The bad news is that your current events probably do not all have all the information that I have shown here, or the information present in each event is not sufficient to allow it to be automatically processed. Part of your job during the ServiceNow implementation is to make the appropriate changes in your environment so that all the events do contain the appropriate amount of operational data and that they are being processed correctly. Simply determining the definition of "processed correctly" for each event will be one of the largest challenges you face in your implementation.

Section B: Organizational Information

This section dives into the background and needs of your organization. In my opinion, this is the most important factor in any implementation of any ServiceNow application. My goal in this section is to give you information about the questions you need to ask of your organization to help make your implementation successful. This background information is critically important to the success of your rollout, and it is almost always overlooked to some degree.

The details of any organization are unique, and you need to acknowledge that fact. With the number of different frameworks available (ITIL, TOGAF, COBIT, etc.), many people believe that there should be similarities between the processes used in different organizations. The truth is that every corporation does things in their own incredibly unique way. You may find some high-level similarities, but those all disappear when you get into the details. I have been implementing event management systems for over two decades, at over two hundred customers, and no two are alike. Each implementation has been customized extensively.

The chapters included in this section are:

5. What is Your Goal?

6. Where are You Now?

7. Your Current Tickets

8. Analyze Your Existing Event Management System

9. Present Your Findings

10. Unhelpful Questions

11. What is Your Vision for How ServiceNow Will be Used?

12. Training, training, training!

13. CMDB

14. Prove Replication of Existing Functionality First

15. Be Prepared to Show off Capabilities as They are Implemented

16. Success Depends on Education and Adoption

17. Continuous Improvement

5   What is Your Goal?

While this seems like a straightforward question, your answer will usually have some number of nuances that are unique to your environment. While you think about your specific plans for your ServiceNow ITOM rollout, I will give you a few examples of goals that my clients have come up with.

When dealing with a large enterprise containing legacy systems, there really is no such thing as a right or wrong answer. There is no one specific recommendation that can be applied in all situations. Every single company has its own unique mix of capabilities and constraints that shape its decisions. It is also important to note that ServiceNow ITOM is not the only IT system you need for managing your company's IT operations. It has a ton of functionality, but it will be just one of the numerous applications and platforms in your IT portfolio.

5.1   *Keep Existing System for Now, But All New Events Go to ServiceNow ITOM*

There is no right or wrong way forward, and this choice is as valid as any others. Here are the relevant factors in play at this particular client that influenced this decision:

1. Established event management system that has been in place for over a decade.
2. Tons of customization to the event management rules and integrations with existing systems.
3. Numerous integration points in the environment sending events to the existing event management system.
4. Multiple related systems are planned to be phased out over time.
5. There have been rumors that the event management system will be retired, but no verification of this rumor.
6. New monitoring and log management systems are being newly implemented in different parts of the organization, and these have never been integrated with the existing event management system.
7. The existing ticketing system is being replaced by ServiceNow.
8. No clear direction or authorization around event management has been stated by management.
9. Multiple groups are frustrated with desired functions that are missing in the current event management system.

Looking at all of these factors together led me to recommend that this client keep their existing system for now, but to send all new events directly to ServiceNow through new integrations. While the path may not seem like the most optimal, I believe it was the best way forward for this organization.

5.2   Keep Existing System, Integrate with ServiceNow ITOM

This is like the previous client's goal, but with the decision to keep the current event management system in place. The following are some of the factors that influenced this decision.

1.   A long-term license was recently signed for the existing event management system.
2.   The current event management system provides valuable capabilities such as root cause analysis, impact analysis and useful situational awareness.
3.   All stakeholders are happy with the operation of the current event management system, but they see that many operational efficiencies can be achieved with ServiceNow (particularly in the area of managed and monitored orchestration activities).
4.   ServiceNow will be replacing the existing ticketing system.
5.   ServiceNow will provide a Service Catalog function, which will be a completely new capability for this company.
6.   There are published, well-defined integrations into the existing event management system, and those integrations are used by all teams in the organization.

As you can see, this customer had its own unique set of factors to consider. Their particular situation led them to choose to simply integrate with the existing system. As in the previous example, I believe this customer made the correct choice based on their specific configuration and requirements.

This is the scenario covered in the Case Study at the end of this book.

5.3   Move All Event Management to Splunk and ServiceNow ITOM

This is a much larger change than either of the previous two examples. The following are some of the organizational characteristics that prompted this decision.

1.   A large Splunk purchase was recently made, with the goal of centralizing all log management in Splunk.
2.   Many groups are unsatisfied with the capabilities provided by the current event management tool.
3.   The current ticketing tool will be replaced by ServiceNow.

4. Any changes to the current system are slow and painful to implement, so a wholesale change to an entirely different system is seen as the best path.
5. Operators currently have no situational awareness when a ticket is assigned to them; all they see is a minimal amount of data in the ticket.
6. Management sees that most or all the current IT processes are outdated and overly complicated, so they want to rework everything using ServiceNow capabilities wherever possible.

Again, I think this was the right decision for this customer. With their legacy system, they were extremely inefficient. It was easily recognized by management that a complete change was needed, and they took their purchase of ServiceNow as the impetus to undergo a digital transformation.

5.4 Move All Event Management to ServiceNow

This goal is like the example above, but it has some shortcomings that I will discuss after reviewing the factors that influenced their decision.

1. Many groups are unsatisfied with the capabilities provided by the current event management tool.
2. The current ticketing tool will be replaced by ServiceNow.
3. Any changes to the current system are slow and painful to implement, so a wholesale change to an entirely different system is seen as the best path.
4. Operators currently have no situational awareness when a ticket is assigned to them; all they see is a minimal amount of data in the ticket.
5. Management sees that most or all the current IT processes are outdated and overly complicated, so they want to rework everything using ServiceNow capabilities wherever possible.

These factors are **almost** identical to the previous example, with the exclusion of Splunk. This is the only decision of the four I have presented here that I believe is not quite complete. Specifically, I know that this company will have to invest in a data storage solution to store the large number of events that are generated in their environment. ServiceNow is great at many functions, but it is not great as an ad-hoc reporting system dealing with hundreds of millions of event records. That is not a knock on ServiceNow by any means, but rather a recognition of what it can and cannot do. I know that this customer will want to retain at least a year of historical events for reporting purposes (around 500 million events), and ServiceNow just is not built for this particular purpose. Specifically, Events in ServiceNow are meant to be temporary messages that are used for tactical operations (break-fix, for example). The **em_event** table is not meant to store scores of old, dormant events.

5.5 *Some combination of all the above and more.*

Realistically, this is the choice you will most likely end up with. You need to be flexible with your goals because there are a lot of unknowns in any ServiceNow ITOM implementation. You need to assess each new requirement or need as it emerges and deal with it appropriately.

6   Where Are You Now?

A ServiceNow solution is sold to executives as the solution to all the company's problems. Search for their "Let's workflow it" commercials from Fall of 2020 to see examples of this. What is amazing is that the ServiceNow platform actually has the capabilities and is customizable enough to make good on this sales pitch. The big caveat in this situation is that you need to know where you are now and at least have an idea of the future steps that will lead you to your ideal future state. The first difficult challenge in this process is identifying the current state of each of your tools/functions/departments that will be managed via ServiceNow.

The driving force behind a ServiceNow purchase is some number of stakeholders complaining that the current processes do not meet all of their needs. While this statement is often valid, what is usually missing is a detailed description of the current state of IT operations management in the organization. The processes you have in place now, no matter how ugly, are keeping your IT systems up and operational. There are highly likely some parts of the process that make life easy and other parts that are challenging. Defining your current state in the form of process diagrams or flowcharts is critical to having a successful ServiceNow implementation.

As one of the first steps in a ServiceNow ITOM Health implementation, you need to make a brutally honest assessment of exactly where you are now with monitoring and event management in your enterprise. Ideally, you want a tech savvy business process analyst assigned to this task. Below are some of the questions that need to be answered. The answers to these questions will likely be extremely painful and will likely draw criticism from management. There is no good way around that, so you need to be prepared for that eventuality.

6.1   Do you have a centrally managed event management system that receives messages from all monitoring tools and is used to open tickets and send notifications?

This may seem like an extremely basic question, but it's one that deserves an answer. At most of my clients, the answer has normally been something like "Yes, pretty much". That answer means that there are some loose ends in the process that need to be identified and tidied up. Moving to a new system requires complete knowledge (in the form of diagrams and documents) of the current processes in place.

6.2   Do you have individual monitoring tools that are sending alerts to the appropriate teams without opening tickets?

Every company I have worked with has some number of teams that are doing their own thing outside of the central event management and ticketing systems. It appears to be just a fact of life that these exist. You need to find these rogue systems and work with them to integrate into your new ServiceNow environment. These teams are currently operating outside of any kind of oversight, which too often leads to outages that cannot easily be resolved.

6.3   Do you have a mishmash of monitoring tools and event management systems deployed throughout your environment?

The answer to this question is usually Yes for my clients. This happens over time based on reorganizations, inconsistent governance, or any number of other reasons. To get the most out of your new ServiceNow implementation, you need to identify these tools and their owners, and do everything you can to make ServiceNow ITOM the system of record for Events and Incidents.

6.4   Do you have no idea what is actually happening with regards to monitoring and event management in your environment?

Unfortunately, this is the true situation in organizations far too often. Reorganizations and decoupled decentralization of functions allows the proliferation of completely disparate tools and processes. If this is your current state, then wrangling all of this into your ServiceNow ITOM implementation is going to take quite a bit of hard work. If this is the scenario in your organization, it is extremely important to let management know this because it will have a large impact on the time and money involved in your implementation.

6.5   What are the current capabilities that your customers/operators rely on?

In addition to identifying all your different user groups, you need to define the capabilities that they rely on. Some examples of capabilities that they may currently have are:

- per-event ticket assignment

- per-event emails

- per-event SMS text

- per-event script (remediation action)

- what else?

This is a good time to introduce one concept of Agile Project Management: User Stories. User

Stories are remarkably similar to requirements, but they provide additional details beyond what would normally be found in a requirement. For example, a user story could be:

"As a Network Operations Center operator, when I look at my group's tickets, I see the hostname associated with each. Our naming standard is defined such that the first three characters of the host name tell me the data center or location of the impacted host or device. I use that information, along with my knowledge of the importance of our different locations, to determine the priority of the ticket compared to others."

This user story gives information about what data needs to be presented to this user in any new system and how the data is actually being used. Note that this story uncovers a "hidden" calculation that is being performed: the operator is determining the priority of the ticket based on some tribal knowledge that is not actually implemented in the system. As part of your implementation, you need to flush out as many of these hidden calculations and tribal knowledge as possible so they can be documented and codified in ServiceNow ITOM.

6.6 Are you happy with the tickets that are opened now?
You're probably replacing your ticketing system, so now is an opportune time to audit your existing ticketing system and all of the tickets it creates. You will likely find that not all tickets are actually important. I will cover this topic in more detail in the chapter named Your Current Tickets.

6.7 Do you have a CMDB?
My guess is that at least 95% of people reading this do not have an actual CMDB. Even if you do, it is not in a format compatible with Service Now, and it may not be worth the effort to try to map the data to the ServiceNow CMDB. To create your CMDB, you need to use ServiceNow Discovery to the fullest extent possible. You will probably need to also load data manually, and that's normal, especially for data like System Owner, or Business Application, etc.

The most important point I want to stress is that you need to use the ServiceNow Discovery capability for as much as possible. This function will help you quickly build the technical part of your CMDB.

7 Your Current Tickets

Since you are planning to replace your existing ticketing system with ServiceNow, you need a complete audit of your current ticket system, in addition to your event management system. You need to identify exactly how the system is used and the activities that users perform within the tool. You need this information to ensure that your ServiceNow ITOM implementation provides at least these same capabilities.

Some of the questions you need to answer as part of this audit are below.

7.1 Is the ticketing system simply a place to store information?

In other words, are tickets opened simply to record the fact that something happened in the environment?

In ServiceNow, each Incident or Service Request represents something in the environment that must be addressed within a reasonable service window. Alerts exist in ServiceNow ITOM to show that something is wrong and should be addressed. I discuss the difference between Events, Alerts, and Incidents later in the book.

7.2 Should each current ticket equate to an Incident in ServiceNow?

The answer to this question is ALWAYS "no". You can try to convince yourself otherwise, but you would be wrong. Use the implementation of ServiceNow ITOM as an opportunity to cull some of the non-actionable tickets that are currently being created in your legacy ticketing system.

7.3 Do multiple teams have tickets created for similar issues?

For example, the OS team wants to be notified when any drive on a Windows server is more than 98% full, and an application team wants to be notified when the D: drive is 95% full.

There is no generic way to resolve this in ServiceNow. It can be solved in one of any number of ways, but you first need to identify all (or many) of your users' needs before you can develop a useful implementation.

7.4 What are all the ways that tickets are opened today?

Manually?

From the event management system?

Directly from monitoring tools via an API?

Since you plan on replacing your ticketing system, you need to define all of the ways that tickets are being created today. Your implementation plan needs to handle all of these sources in ServiceNow.

7.5   What data is provided when the ticket is opened vs. what data is added by the ticketing system?

Are there any lookups or transformations performed by the ticketing system?

- o For example, for programmatically-opened tickets is the exact name of the assignment group provided, or does the ticketing system look that data up in a table somewhere?

What is the data that is being looked up? And where does it reside?

- o You do not know if this data will need to be imported into ServiceNow at this point, but you definitely need to identify this data and its source to help make that decision.

Again, you need to identify everything going on in your current ticketing system so that you can intelligently emulate or change that behavior in ServiceNow. You may want to identify these current capabilities in a spreadsheet, or in Atlassian Jira, ServiceNow Visual Task Boards, or any other format that is understandable and consumable by your implementation team and your organization.

7.6   What are the rules governing ticket creation?

Can a ticket be opened for any reason at all, or does a ticket need to represent an impacted service of some type? What processes are kicked off once an Incident is opened?

7.7   Do tickets represent both service requests and problems in the environment?

ServiceNow ITOM separates these into different types of tickets. An alarm in the environment may create an Incident ticket, but a Service Request ticket should only be created via the ServiceNow Service Catalog.

7.8   Exactly how are operators and engineers processing tickets today?

You need to document the processes in place today that are used by the user community to handle tickets. The exact workflow of both operators and engineers must be documented fully to ensure that this is completely understood. In this context, I am using the term "operator" to refer to a first-level responder and "engineer" to refer to a second- or third-level responder. To ensure a successful implementation, the daily work processes of both groups need to be fully documented.

8   Analyze Your Existing Event Management System

This may seem almost redundant to mention, but you need to deeply analyze your current event management system, specifically including the events that are currently being processed in the environment. I recommend initially taking a complete export of at least 30 days of events (including ALL columns) into an Excel workbook so you can get an idea of what you are working with. The main purpose of this analysis is to find the answers to several questions. 30 days of data is a good place to start, but you will eventually want to look at a full year of data to catch as many periodic events as possible.

In this section I am just defining the first few nodes from the ITIL Event Management diagram presented earlier. Specifically, I am describing this part of the diagram.

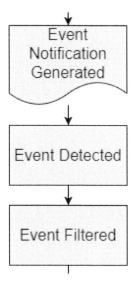

Figure 8-1 Portion of ITIL Event Management covered in this section

Some of the more common questions that need to be answered during this audit are described in the sections that follow.

8.1   *Identify the people with deep knowledge of the current system*

Knowing how the existing system is paramount to a successful migration. And that means all aspects of the "current system". Normally, your legacy system does not have strict functional boundaries like ServiceNow provides. This means that there will not be a one-to-one mapping of current responsibilities to responsibilities in ServiceNow. This fact must be understood by all interested parties, and time must be allotted for meetings to define these new sets of responsibilities and for all team members to get up-to-speed on the new technologies and functions they will need to perform in ServiceNow.

8.2   How are alarms generated and sent to our system?

You need to identify all the ways that alarm messages are generated and sent to your existing event management system. At some point, I recommend that you document this information in the form of a diagram. This diagram will be the center of numerous discussions throughout your implementation, so creating it is extremely important. I strongly recommend **draw.io** for this purpose. The following is an example of a high-level diagram of an organization's monitoring infrastructure, including the event management system and the ticketing system.

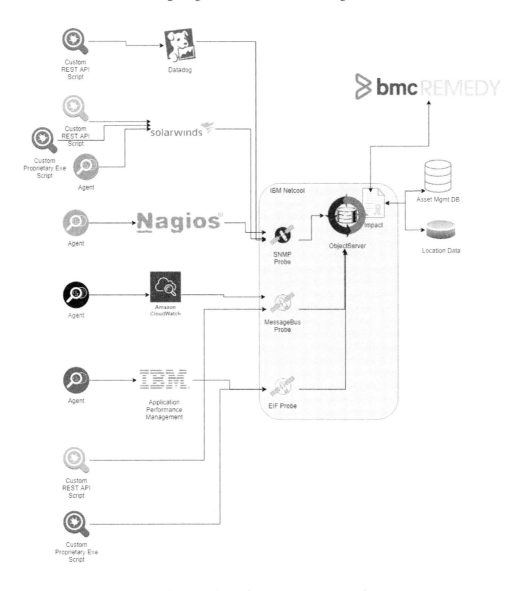

Figure 8-2 Monitoring and event management architecture

That architecture is a very high-level representation of what is going on. To be thorough, you need to make a sub-diagram for each component, where that sub-diagram explains the format, capabilities and challenges associated with that component in your environment.

You may already have such a diagram in your environment, though many organizations do not. Even a simple diagram like this can really help everyone in the project understand the scope of monitoring in the environment.

8.3   What information is contained in the raw messages?

If you have no plans to replace your existing event management system, you can skip over this part. I believe it contains some useful information, but it is not immediately important to you if you aren't going to replace your current system.

It is especially important to document the contents and format of the messages that are currently being sent into your event management system if you plan to replace the system in the future. You need to know what kinds of data you are dealing with. It is important to document this for the current and future systems.

In addition to simply documenting the current state of your monitoring infrastructure, another goal of this exercise is to illuminate any important data that does not currently exist in the messages. For example, several of my clients have had monitoring in place that generated inconsistently-formatted messages that did not contain a usable CI name. It was not a problem before implementing ServiceNow ITOM, but it quickly became apparent that it would be a huge problem during the implementation. Because every customer is unique, a different solution was devised for each environment. You will most likely encounter a similar problem, and you want to identify it as early as possible.

8.4   Exactly what processing is done in our event management system?

Even if you have no plans to replace your existing event management system, I think you will get some benefit from reading this section.

This topic may require multiple large diagrams to fully capture the important details. Most organizations I have worked with have had very customized event management systems in place which had been customized by multiple people over multiple years or even decades. You need to document the processing performed not only for your own use, but also to present to stakeholders to help them understand the scope of effort that will be required if the system (or any part of it) is to be replaced.

A great example of a complex event management system is IBM Netcool. This system allows customized scripting at three different locations, each with different capabilities.

Probes:
Process one event at a time and maintain no state.
Provide for text replacement and simple lookups along with if..then..else.
External files can be accessed, but no databases or remote data.

OMNIbus:

In-memory event database.

Scripting has access to all events, allowing for aggregation.

Timer and event-based triggers allowed.

External files can be accessed, but no databases or remote data.

Impact:

Full event enrichment capabilities, including remote databases, REST API calls, etc.

Timer-based policies available.

Policies have access to all events.

Policies can be triggered via external programs.

In such an environment, it could be that you need to document the event processing using a combination of diagrams and documents. It really depends on the complexity of each piece. In producing the documentation, you will likely perform quite a bit of re-work as you identify new patterns and recognize which pieces of code are more important.

8.5   Which field(s) identify different types of events?

The best way to answer this question is to use Excel Pivot Tables. A Pivot Table allows you to group events based on the values in one or more columns and will calculate the number of events in each group. Additionally, I feel strongly that you should share this Excel workbook with everyone involved in the project and ask them to perform their own analysis. Having multiple people analyzing the data will usually lead to the identification of patterns that might otherwise remain hidden.

8.6   Which types of events are the most common?

Answering this question will help guide you toward the events that have the highest priority as far as Event Rules go. There may be other factors that influence the prioritization, but the key is that you must determine some sort of priority order for dealing with the events in your environment. The reason behind this is that your events likely are quite different from each other, and each different type will require the creation of one or more Event Rules. It would be great if all your different event types are all similar enough that they can be handled within a single Event Rule in ServiceNow ITOM, but that's not the norm. The normal case is that every type of event is different enough to require a different Event Rule for processing.

8.7   Which groups are responsible for each type of ticket?

Most often, your primary goal with your event management and ticketing systems has been to simply determine who to assign the eventual ticket to, so gathering this information is a key prerequisite to your implementation of ServiceNow ITOM. The concept of Configuration Items (CIs) and associated assignment/support groups may be a new concept in your organization. As with your existing system in ServiceNow ITOM, getting incidents assigned to the correct groups will be of utmost importance.

9   Present Your Findings

Once you have gone through the discovery exercises described in the previous sections, you need to gather your findings into a format that is appropriate for the different audiences involved with the implementation. The two most likely broad audiences you will have are Executive Management and Technical Groups. Some of the differences between these two groups are described here.

9.1   *Executive Management*

Presentations to executives should be at a high level and should identify the organizational concerns that have been uncovered. These presentations should be used to help assign the appropriate people or groups to work on any issues that were found.

9.2   *Technical Groups*

The format for technical groups should dive further into the technical details of the processes that were discovered and should attempt to find answers to any technical questions that remain unanswered.

9.3   *Sample Slides*

The pictures in this section are examples of slides that I have shown in different presentations to communicate the findings of my investigations. The purpose of including them here is to give you ideas about how you might present information that uncover in your own environment. You need to present your findings clearly, so that your audience can consume the information and help you move forward with the implementation

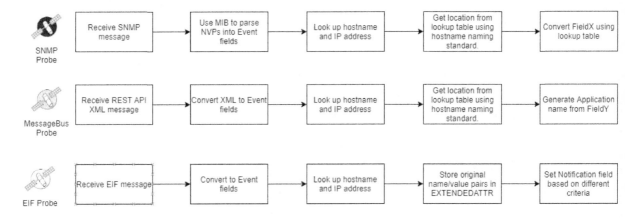

Figure 9-1 Probe event processing

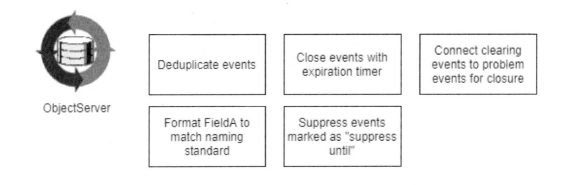

Figure 9-2 ObjectServer event processing

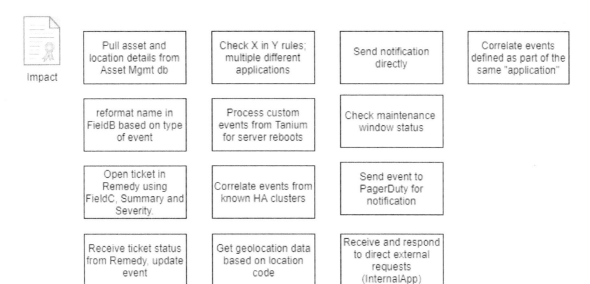

Figure 9-3 Netcool Impact event processing

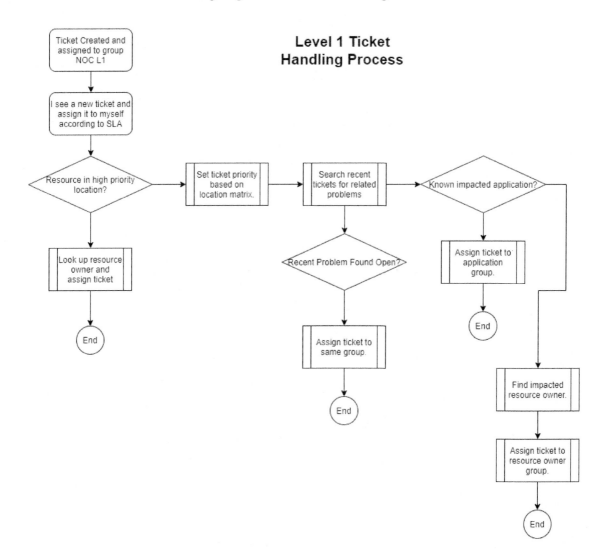

Figure 9-4 Level 1 ticket handling process

10 Unhelpful questions

I have been involved in some number of ServiceNow ITOM implementations where the people leading the project have had little background in monitoring or event management. Basically, they were business or process analysts, but with little domain knowledge. This led to some frustration in these projects because effort was wasted trying to answer questions that were not helpful. I am using this section to point out some of those questions and to explain why they are unhelpful so that you can avoid them in your implementations.

10.1 What kinds of monitors are in use?

This question is not useful because the answer does not provide any useful information. One problem with this question is that each monitoring system usually has its own definition of a "monitor", and a single "monitor" in one system may equate to multiple "monitors" in a different system.

It turned out that the goal of this question was to start analyzing the Events in the environment. See the previous section named **Analyze Your Existing Events** for more information on this topic.

10.2 What different types of CIs are being monitored?

The main problem with this question was the timing of when it was posed to me during an implementation. When it was asked, the organization had not yet developed a common definition for the term **CI**. Some people considered servers to be the only kind of CI, while others considered a CI to be an individual file system or process. Either definition can work, but that definition must be adopted before this question can possibly be answered.

Another problem with this question is that every enterprise is monitoring hundreds or thousands of different types of CIs (if we consider a CI to be a very granular entity like a file, network port, or firewall rule). The ServiceNow platform has extremely specific names for each type of CI (e.g., cmdb_ci_batch_job, cmdb_ci_file_system, etc.), and there is no documented mapping between ServiceNow CI types and those of your organization.

I believe that a better version of this question is:

"What are the impacted resources that are causing events to be generated?"

Again, this goes back to analyzing your current events. The monitors are important because they generate the events, but the events themselves need to be analyzed.

11 What is Your Vision for How ServiceNow Will be Used?

The marketing material looks great, but you need to have a concrete idea about how your organization will use ServiceNow ITOM for dealing with Alerts and Incidents when the implementation is actually put into production. A lofty goal of "leveraging service maps to identify the root cause of any problem in the environment" is nice-sounding dream, but it contains no information about how users will interact with the application on Day One.

11.1 How do your users want to use the application on Day One?

This question is extremely important for adoption. The ServiceNow user interface, combined with its powerful business logic, will allow your users to do virtually anything. That flexibility is amazing, but you need to work with your users to define exactly how the product will be used in your organization. You need to fully describe how you initially plan to have your users interact with the product.

Work with your different user groups to define as many User Stories as possible. The product can do anything, but its success in your organization comes down to how it meets the needs of your users. The Service Request and HR components of ServiceNow get lots of attention from business process analysts, but ITOM operators are often left to fend for themselves. That is one of the factors that drove me to write this book – there is not enough information available on how Operations Center users are supposed to do their jobs in a completely new system.

11.2 Agent Workspace

The Agent Workspace is most likely the interface you want your operators to use as their primary dashboard.

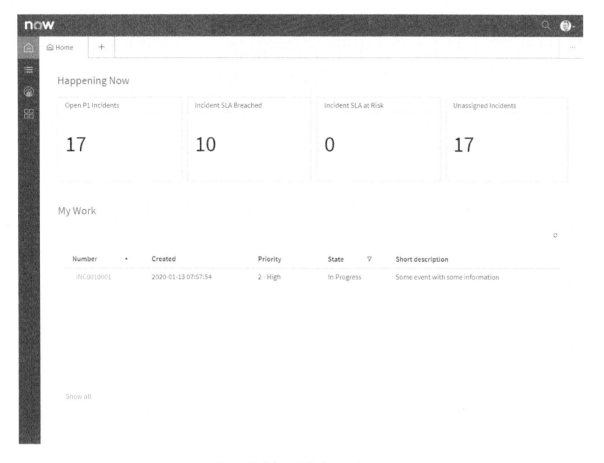

Figure 11-1 Agent Workspace home

The Agent Workspace home by default shows some amount of useful information, but it normally requires customization in every implementation. When migrating from another system to ServiceNow ITOM, I find that operators are usually most interested in viewing the list of Incidents and/or Alerts that are assigned to their group. As the system matures in your environment, operators can be introduced to Service Views and other features, but in every implementation I've worked on, operators need a list of their work items on Day One.

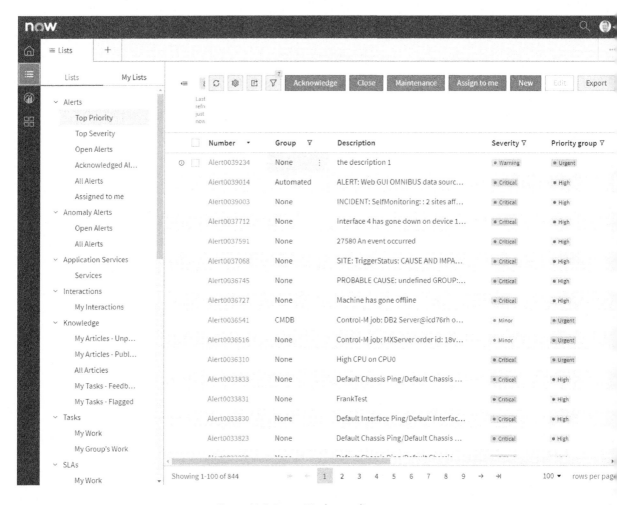

Figure 11-2 Agent Workspace lists

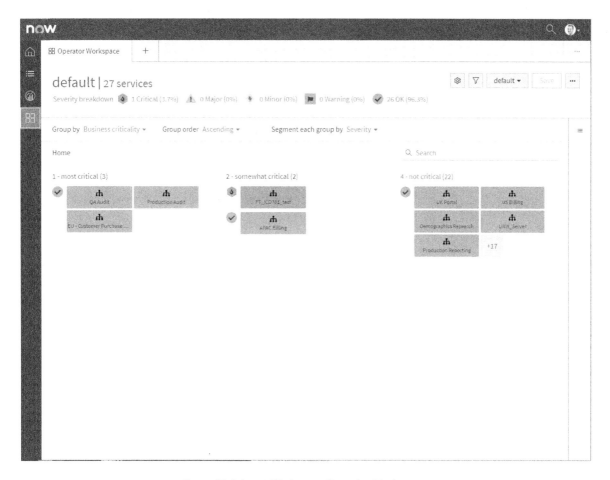

Figure 11-3 Agent Workspace Operator Workspace

In your environment, you need to work with your operators to define exactly when they would use each of the above screens and the exact steps they need to take to perform their job functions. This information can and should be developed collaboratively with the different groups of operators. To start that collaboration, however, you will need to define specific use cases **using your organization's event data** to show them how they can resolve problems.

You need to show to your operators at least three to five examples of every step they would take within the tool to solve a specific problem. For example:

1. Your shift starts and you log into the Agent Workspace at
    http://myinstance@service-now.com/now/workspace/agent/home

2. You see that there are 17 unassigned incidents.
3. You click on the Unassigned Incidents widget to view the list of incidents.
4. You then sort by Priority to find the highest priority unassigned incidents.
5. Look for one that you might be familiar with, starting from highest to lowest priority, and assign it to yourself to work on.
6. The Agent Assist pane of the Incident Details should show at least one Knowledge Article for this incident.
7. Read the Knowledge Article and perform the actions documented.

While the above set of steps may seem straightforward, you must remember that this is a completely new tool with different capabilities than the previous system. You will need to go over these steps (and two to four more examples at least) multiple times with multiple groups to get everyone familiar with the new process flow that they will be using to do their work.

And speaking of process flow, you really need to provide a diagram or slideshow or video of each of these sets of steps. This will be used to train both the existing operators and new hires. Having graphical documentation of exactly what steps to take and what to do when something goes wrong will greatly reduce the amount of time required to onboard new operators.

11.3 Agile is key

Your implementation team needs to fully understand the intricacies of the Agile Methodology. The leader of the project must be well versed in Agile project management and in Event Management and monitoring. This person must also understand that their knowledge must be passed on to everyone else involved in the project.

A successful ServiceNow implementation is a continuously modified process. In most organizations, ServiceNow is the central tool in the Continuous Service Improvement initiative. Though it is a continuous process, new functionality needs to be rolled out to users regularly, and this is where Agile comes into the picture. Using the Agile Methodology, you release new functionality every few weeks. There are tons of details, along with deciding on Scrum vs Kanban, but it boils down to regularly (every 2-4 weeks) releasing new functionality. This is very different from the traditional Waterfall model, where a team works for a long time to produce a single large deliverable. Agile allows your users to submit new requests regularly, which ensures that they can meet any new challenges they encounter.

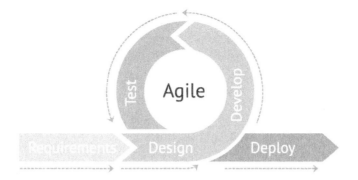

Figure 11-4 Agile Project Cycle

12 Training, training, training!

The stakeholders and users of the system need to understand not just its capabilities, but exactly how they will be expected to interact with the ServiceNow user interface. Moving from a legacy system will, by design, introduce more changes than you can imagine. Eventually, every one of these changes will be seen as an improvement over your current system, but the only way to get there is through the education of the users.

To this end, a successful implementation will need to produce tens or even hundreds of environment-specific videos that provide details about how the system should be used at your organization. The easiest way to start this process is to identify questions that users are asking, then create videos that provide the answers to those questions. You can create a web page in the format of an FAQ, for example, where each answer is a short video. Now that your company has purchased ServiceNow, it is certain to be a huge part of your business processes for many years to come. ServiceNow will become the backbone of a number of your business processes, and it won't be going away any time soon. Keeping this in mind, you want to ensure that users can easily find instructional videos on your intranet to help them easily navigate the product.

Training and knowledge transfer are also extremely important to the implementation team and the team that will be supporting the system after the initial implementation is complete. In addition to regular meetings, all of the changes to the system need to be clearly documented. A project management system like Atlassian Jira can be a great help with this responsibility.

13 CMDB

The concept of a CMDB (Configuration Management Database) has been around since the 1980s, but most companies simply have not implemented one yet. The reason for this slow adoption is that it is extremely difficult. In the early days, it was easy to blame the tools for the problem, but now with products like ServiceNow, the tools have all the capabilities you could possibly need, which, for better or worse, illuminates the likelihood that it's a problem with operational processes.

To get the most out of ServiceNow ITOM, you need to have a valid, current, updated and maintained CMDB. The best way to accomplish this is to use ServiceNow Discovery. No matter how much buy-in you have from all levels of your organization, this is going to take a long time. That is an established fact. To implement discovery, ServiceNow will need to have access to service accounts on each of the systems to be discovered, and this is where the objections will begin.

The product documentation covering discovery is extensive, so I am not covering that in this book. However, I do have what I believe is some particularly important information about the organizational barriers that you will encounter while implementing discovery.

13.1 *Implementing Discovery will take a long time*

The discovery capability of ServiceNow is one of the most comprehensive in the industry. It is also surprisingly easy to configure. The problem in a large enterprise is that it needs to be granted access to systems and applications that are managed by multiple different groups. And this required access must usually be approved by not only the group responsible for administration, but also one or more central security groups. To make matters worse, these different groups usually report to different directors in the organization, and those different directors generally do not get along with each other. Normally, each organization has some unique set of obstacles that make the implementation extremely difficult.

My main point is to increase your estimate for the amount of time and effort required to implement ServiceNow ITOM discovery. And by increase, I mean that you should take your estimate, no matter how conservative you think it is, and multiply it by at least eight. You read that right – multiply by **eight** at a minimum. If you think there is no way that it could possibly take more than four months, I am telling you that it will take an absolute minimum of 32 months.

I know that most people reading this book will laugh at this recommendation, but it is based on two decades of experience trying to implement discovery tools from different vendors. The individual tools may have some technical limitations, but those have always been trivial compared to the organizational roadblocks that have come up in every single implementation. As a matter of fact, I know of no implementations where the discovery tool has been allowed to access all of the known systems in the environment. There is always some justification given for why the discovery process cannot possibly be given access to some number of systems. I would love to be proven wrong someday, so I encourage you to email me directly to let me know if you have a different experience.

13.2 CMDB Relationships

It is extremely important for you to completely understand the fundamental concepts of CMDB Relationships so that you can understand the CMDB. There are Relationship Types and Relationships. Each Relationship is a row in the **cmdb_rel_ci** table, which requires a parent CI, a child CI, and a Relationship Type. Before you can create a Relationship, the appropriate Relationship Type must already exist as a row in the **cmdb_rel_type** table. A Relationship Type specifies a **Parent descriptor** and a **Child descriptor**. A descriptor is used to specify the relationship from the perspective of the Relationship-specific parent or child. Relationship governance rules define the types of CIs that can be specified as a parent or as a child in each Relationship Type. Relationship governance rules are generally specified using the CI Class Manager. There are around 50 Relationship Types defined by default in Event Management in the Paris release, and more can be added. When specifying a Relationship between two CIs, the descriptor you use depends on the first CI mentioned. For example, the following statement can be used to describe one relationship between the Tomcat server "tomcat-server1" and the Linux server "linux-host01":

> tomcat-server1 'Runs on' linux-host01

In this case, "tomcat-server1" is the child in the Relationship, so the Child descriptor "Runs on" is used. If we want to state this same relationship from the perspective of the Linux server, you can use the statement:

> linux-host01 'Runs' tomcat-server1

In this case, the Parent descriptor "Runs" is used.

Exactly what each Relationship Type means or how it is used can be found in the product documentation.

An important point to make is that there is no such thing as a universal "parent/child" relationship between two CIs. This is an extremely common misunderstanding, and that is why I'm making such a big point about it. When you talk about a Relationship, you are specifically talking about a specific Relationship Type between two (and only two) CIs. When you specify the Relationship, you use the descriptor of the Relationship Type that is associated with the first CI you mention (e.g., "Runs on" vs "Runs"). The Relationship Types that come by default with the system are used for specific purposes. You can define additional Relationship Types if needed, but you need to ensure you fully understand all the concepts related to Relationship Types and Relationships before doing so.

14 Prove Replication of Existing Functionality First

New technology makes people think they can immediately solve the hardest problems in their environment. This is a disastrously incorrect assumption 99% of the time. Your users have a lot of existing expectations that took years or decades to develop. Don't ignore these needs. Basically, you need to emulate the existing system capabilities, while working to implement your ideal future state. Ideally/eventually, you want to merge the two. The best way to do that is to allow users to see both implementations – the replicated/"Old" environment and the "New" one.

Gather information from your users about exactly how they use the product so that you can replicate that behavior in the new system. ServiceNow ITOM is a huge new system, and your users need to know that it can at very least provide them with the capabilities that currently exist. One goal of the implementation is probably to create new processes, and that will occur over time. In the first part of your implementation, you need to prove to your users that this new system provides the basic functions that they are used to.

15 Be Prepared to Show Off Capabilities as They are Implemented.

This is related to Agile project management. As you implement functionality in ServiceNow, you need to demonstrate those new functions to your user community and ask them for feedback. As you are replicating existing functionality, that is what you need to demonstrate to your users. Operators in the NOC generally do not care about pie-in-the-sky possibilities; what they care about is resolving problems as quickly as possible.

Some capabilities that will eventually be of interest to your Operators are:

- Impact analysis

- Service impacting view

- Agent workspace

You should be ready to show off these capabilities in any meeting/training.

16 Success Depends on Education and Adoption.

You MUST show each group the product capabilities **with the data that each group is interested in**. There are tons of videos on the Internet that show "the art of the possible" with ServiceNow, but you need to demonstrate how each different group will actually interact with the product at your company. To do this, you must use your company's data. This is the only way to ensure that audience members can experience and evaluate their individual processes within the product. People are busy and worried about their specific responsibilities. They do not have time to extrapolate what they might do based on unrelated data.

As you can imagine, you need to do lots of research before your first large-scale presentation. You need to know how different users are using the current (legacy) product and you need to know what they're actually trying to accomplish. With these two pieces of data, the hope is that you can marry the two and encourage adoption of ServiceNow.

Even more important than the users, you need to ensure that the implementation team receives the education needed to successfully implement ServiceNow. Exactly what education is needed and in what format depends on each individual on the team, but the fact is that everyone on the implementation team needs to be extremely well-versed in the technical aspects of ServiceNow.

17 Move to a service management mindset.

The term IT Service Management has been around for a long time, but most organizations still think in terms of individual servers. Moving to a service management mindset requires that people discuss issues in terms of the impacted services. In general, this will require pictures or diagrams of some sort. Happily, ServiceNow allows you to create service mapping diagrams based on discovered data in your enterprise. Very often, the team responsible for a particular service already has an idea of what the service looks like, whether that's depicted in an actual diagram or not. One of the goals of ServiceNow is to provide enterprise visibility to the IT infrastructure, so that even the newest team member has immediate access to the tools to help resolve problems (or at least to route the problem to the responsible party). For example, here is a Service Dependency View of the Bond Trading application in ServiceNow:

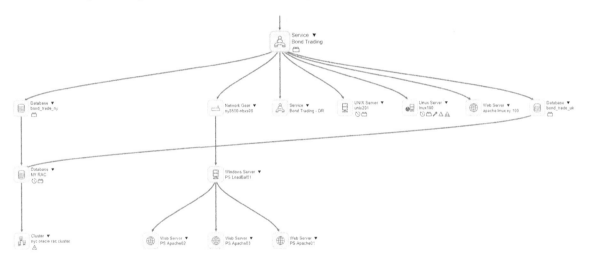

Figure 17-1 Service Dependency View

This diagram makes it extremely easy to see all the components that make up a service, and it allows the user to immediately see which component is impacted by an Alert or Incident. Working with these diagrams makes quick work of impact analysis and root cause analysis. Without this kind of diagram, when an incident is assigned to an operator, generally all that operator knows is the text of the incident and the host that encountered the problem that caused the incident to be created. Having a dependency diagram also makes it easy to describe each service or application to a new operator, developer or engineer.

In ServiceNow ITOM, Services (Technical or Application) can be subscribed to. This means that when an Incident or Alert is created that affects a Service, all subscribers will be notified. To me this is a powerful capability, but I have found that most operators do not share my enthusiasm because the organization has not migrated to a service management mindset. This means that operators are using some other information (usually some type of tribal knowledge) to prioritize tickets as they are created in the system. Configuring all the prerequisite components to allow these operators to move to a service management framework is a huge part of any implementation, and it usually takes a lot of work.

18 Continuous Improvement

No ServiceNow ITOM implementation is ever truly complete. This means that the system will constantly be updated as your business processes change, or as your processes improve, or as different groups decide to use the tool. Numerous models exist to give you a framework for continually improving the quality of any initiative, and they are all based on the PDCA (Plan-Do-Check-Act) Cycle.

Figure 18-1 Plan-Do-Check-Act cycle

If your company does not already have a Continuous Improvement process in place, you need to work to help implement one. With any such process, the most important component is the **Check** phase, because this is where the comparison is performed between hope and reality. This phase helps you not only assess if you are progressing, but it also helps you determine if you even defined the correct metrics to evaluate.

The point I want you to take away from this section is that your ServiceNow application implementation will be a never-ending process. You need to have knowledgeable and experienced project managers in place to ensure that this continually evolving application is always headed in the right direction. Because of the constant changes in requirements and desired outcomes, I strongly recommend Agile Project Management as the methodology to use with any implementation of this type.

Section C: ServiceNow Implementation Details

In this section I will cover some of the details of ServiceNow ITOM that are most important to a successful implementation. I do want to stress the fact that the product documentation is extremely thorough in telling you exactly how to perform different tasks. The product documentation does not, however, give you detailed information about why you might choose one option/function over another. The ServiceNow wiki and forums cover some of this information through community-sourced questions and answers, and this book is meant as a complement to all those sources.

The chapters included in this section are:

19. The ServiceNow ITOM Way

20. ServiceNow Event Management Processes

21. Pull Connectors

22. Alert Groups

23. ServiceNow Events Just Contain Data (no references)

24. CI Binding

25. Use A Separate Log Search Platform

26. Ignoring Events

27. Custom Flow Actions

28. What About AIOps?

29 Work on Getting the Correct Information into Alerts

30. Compare Existing Tickets to ServiceNow Incidents

31. Current Processes Need Organizational Exposure

32. Event Table Details

33. Testing Server-side Scripts

34. REST API Explorer

35. Customizing the Transform and Compose Form

19 The ServiceNow ITOM Way

The ServiceNow platform and ServiceNow ITOM are architected in such a way that your specific processes may not be directly implementable in the application. This is where subject matter experts and ServiceNow architects are needed. Without proper guidance, it is very easy for an implementation to become overly complex and unusable due to the amazing flexibility provided by the ServiceNow platform. I have a few tips for you regarding ServiceNow ITOM.

19.1 *Every Alert and Incident should contain a reference to the affected CI.*

CI Binding is very customizable, but you want to follow a consistent pattern when specifying the affected CI. The affected CI may be a host, filesystem, application, or any other object in your CMDB. CI Binding is performed during the process when an **Event Rule** is creating an Alert. There are several sections later in the book that go into the details of this. Having a reference to the affected CI allows you to perform impact analysis and root cause analysis, which help you to accurately triage alerts. The CI **may** also allow you to determine the assignment for the Alert or Incident, but this is not always the case. For example, you may have one filesystem that is used by two different application teams. When a problem in this filesystem causes an Incident to be created, which team should be assigned that Incident? The answer is usually "it depends on the problem", which means that some additional logic and information needs to be leveraged to determine the correct answer. Simply defining the Support Group and/or the Assignment Group for the affected CI in the CMDB does not give you the answer.

19.2 *To build your CMDB, you REALLY need to use ServiceNow Discovery.*

You will always have some data that is manually loaded, and that is OK, but you need to leverage the ServiceNow discovery process as much as possible.

Without Discovery, trying to map your data to the ServiceNow schema is a long, expensive, painful process that will fail 99 times out of 100, regardless of how much time or money you have. There is no detailed documentation on exactly what information is generated by discovery, so you would have to reverse engineer the process to determine the correct mappings. (The product documentation contains a list of all the CMDB tables, but this does not have the gory details about exactly which objects will be mapped to which class.) This reverse engineering would take an exceptionally long time, and ServiceNow could change their implementation at any point, nullifying some or all of your effort.

My point is that you need to leverage Discovery as much as possible.

19.3 A ServiceNow implementation expects that organizational mandates can be made to force everyone to follow ServiceNow processes.

This is key: your business processes MUST change, and there must be a centralized control board that manages these processes. You can bend ServiceNow ITOM to follow any processes that you have defined. However, what you need to do is educate yourself on ITIL processes and ServiceNow ITOM to learn the best practices for organizational processes and then change your processes to follow those best practices more closely. It is extremely easy to defile the standard ServiceNow processes to mirror your own company's outdated processes, but that is not recommended.

The ServiceNow platform works best when you have consistent, orderly, repeatable processes. You should take this opportunity to modify your in-use processes to be orderly and repeatable, with as few exceptions as possible. As strange as it may sound, I am not stating that all of your processes need to be exactly the same; they need to be orderly and repeatable. I know from in-the-trenches experience that you cannot force multiple groups to follow a single, rigid process. However, if your process allows for the definition of group-specific details, you can allow each group to have a customized process at a micro level while still having similarity at a macro level. An example of this can be seen in the Service Catalog. Each type of request is different in some way, and each of these requests may be processed differently, but they all exist in the Service Catalog. This is a difficult concept to explain, and that is why each implementation needs to include very competent process people who can work alongside ServiceNow experts to combine their capabilities to produce an efficient and useful implementation.

19.4 Notifications are likely different than you have configured before.

Notifications are not event- or alert- specific by default. In the Case Study at the end of this book, you will see one way that I have gotten around this.

You can define "normal" notifications as you would with almost any service desk system. By this I mean that you can define conditions under which an email and/or SMS message will be sent to a known group of recipients.

Another capability provided by the ServiceNow platform is the ability to create subscribable notifications. This type of notification is defined exactly like a "normal" notification, plus users can "subscribe" to the notification. This is basically to allow a user to add their name to the recipient list for the notification.

Every CI is "subscribable", but the default is to only send notifications on Incident, Problem or

Change record creation (NOT Alerts). When you subscribe to a CI, it means that you will get notified each time an Incident, Problem or Change that targets the CI is created.

19.5 Investigate everything available before adding fields/columns to tables.

The ServiceNow database is extensive. While it is quite easy to add new tables and fields, that should not be the first customization you think of when encountering a new requirement during an implementation. You should be familiar with the database and the relevant functions available in ServiceNow so that you can choose to leverage an existing capability whenever possible. Leveraging built-in capabilities will allow your instance to run more smoothly and will ensure that upgrades go as smoothly as possible.

19.6 A CMDB With Relationships is Important.

Relationships between CIs are what give you the full picture of the environment when performing impact analysis or root cause analysis. Without these relationships, the CMDB has considerably less value.

20 ServiceNow Event Management Processes

The following diagram shows how a problem in the environment ends up as an Event in ServiceNow and ultimately as an incident.

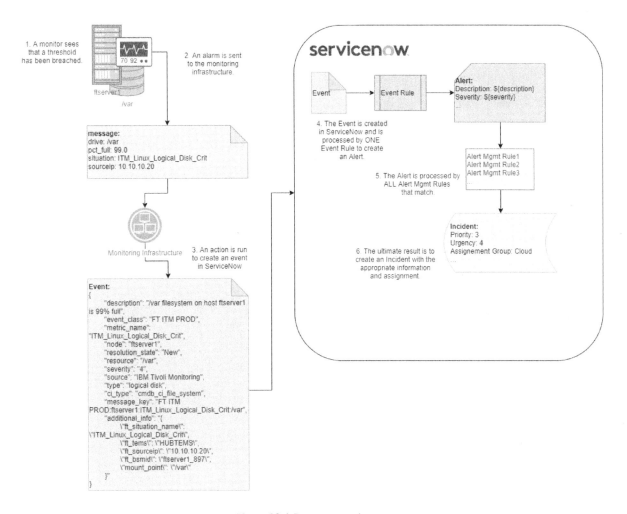

Figure 20-1 Event processing

The above diagram shows the components that make up the Event Management processes that this book is focused on.

20.1 Events, Alerts, and Incidents

Whether you want to create an **Event, Alert** or **Incident** depends on how you want ServiceNow to process the incoming message. In general, you will use a similar REST API to create any one of these. The exception to this general rule is the use of Pull Connectors. A ServiceNow Pull Connector is, essentially, a script that runs on the MID server to pull data from an external source and creates Events in ServiceNow. If you are using a Pull Connector, then that Pull Connector will be creating Events in ServiceNow (you don't get a choice). However, you can choose to use one or more Pull Connectors in conjunction with direct REST API integration in your environment. We will talk more about combining the two later. The following are the important points to consider when choosing between Events, Alerts and Incidents.

20.1.1 Events

If you send an Event to ServiceNow via the REST API, you will be able to leverage Event Rules and Alert Management Rules to perform different operations on that event. Your Event Rules will perform event correlation, and you will be able to provide CI details like the type and name of the CI to bind the Alert to once that alert is created. You can then leverage Alert Management Rules to perform additional actions on the alert.

I recommend that any integrations into ServiceNow ITOM use the Event interface.

Here is an example of a curl command to send an Event directly to a ServiceNow instance:

```
curl "https://YOURINSTANCE.service-now.com/api/global/em/jsonv2" \
--request POST \
--header "Accept:application/json" \
--header "Content-Type:application/json" \
--data "{

  \"records\":
  [
          {
                  \"description\": \"file system /var almost full on host demoui\",
                  \"event_class\": \"Netcool Prod\",
                  \"metric_name\": \"ITM_Linux_Filesystem\",
                  \"node\": \"demoui\",
                  \"resolution_state\": \"New\",
                  \"resource\": \"/var\",
                  \"severity\": \"4\",
                  \"source\": \"IBM Netcool\",
                  \"type\": \"Filesystem\",
```

```
                    \"ci_type\": \"cmdb_ci_file_system\",
                    \"message_key\": \"ITM_Linux_Filesystem:/var:demoui:6\",
                    \"additional_info\": \
\"{ \
\\\"casdRoute\\\": \\\"APP_DCMTM\\\", \
\\\"casdRequired\\\": \\\"1\\\", \
\\\"notifDest\\\": \\\"APP_DCMTM@xyzcorp.com\\\", \
\\\"notifRequired\\\": \\\"1\\\", \
\\\"sn_ci_type\\\": \\\"cmdb_ci_file_system\\\", \
\\\"sn_name\\\": \\\"/dev/sda2\\\", \
\\\"name\\\": \\\"/dev/sda2\\\", \
\\\"xyz_application\\\": \\\"Documentum PR\\\", \
\\\"xyz_assignment_group\\\": \\\"Documentum Support\\\" \
}\"


            }
        ]
}" \
--user 'admin':'PASSWORD'
```

20.1.2 Alerts

If you create an Alert directly in ServiceNow via the REST API, you will either need to provide the **sys_id** of the affected CI in the **cmdb_ci** field, or you will need to write custom code in an Alert Rule to find the CI based on information in the Alert. Specifically, you will be bypassing the Event Rules entirely (which are responsible for CI binding) if you choose to create Alerts directly in ServiceNow. Alert Management Rules will still run against this Alert, and that is where you can write any necessary custom code.

Another caveat of this approach is that the application that is making the REST API call will be responsible for ensuring that multiple Alerts are not created for the same issue. Creating multiple alerts for the same issue causes unnecessary noise for operators, so it should be avoided if possible. This issue doesn't occur if you create Events in ServiceNow. When you create an Event in ServiceNow, an Event Rule will process that event and will automatically de-duplicate any Events that have the same value in the **message_key** field.

You can navigate to the **REST API Explorer** in your ServiceNow developer instance to get more information on this topic.

20.1.3 Incidents

If you create an Incident directly in ServiceNow via the REST API, you will need to provide all of the fields needed in that Incident. For example, you will need to send in the **sys_id** of the affected CI, the name of the assigned group, etc. Creating an Incident directly means that you are completely avoiding all of the Event and Alert processing rules in ServiceNow. This may be exactly what you want, but it may not be. Taking this route means that you get NONE of the built-in Event and Alert correlation or deduplication that is provided by ServiceNow.

20.2 Event Enrichment

In an event management system that is not backed by a CMDB, the process of event enrichment usually involves adding information to the event itself. This is not the case in ServiceNow. In ServiceNow, once an Event is created, it contains all the information that it will ever contain. If an Alert is created or updated due to an Event, the Alert data is updated, but even the Alert will not directly contain as much enriched data as you may be accustomed to seeing. In ServiceNow, most or all of the enriched data is stored in the CMDB, and the Alert simply needs to contain a reference to the appropriate object in the CMDB. That object in the CMDB is the bound CI, a reference to which is stored in the Alert's **cmdb_ci** field. Since the data is stored and managed in the CMDB, you just need to reference that data instead of copying it to each Alert. The implementation of this concept can be confusing at times, especially if you are reviewing your current processes, but you need to have faith that this new structure will produce better results eventually. All the marketing material and demos you see of ServiceNow are really possible to implement, but it takes time and pain to get there.

20.3 Event Rules vs Alert Management Rules

Event Rules and Alert Management Rules provide quite different capabilities. This section is an overview of exactly what you can do with each type of rule.

20.3.1 Event Rules

Most importantly, only ONE Event Rule will be applied to any incoming Event. Once an Event is processed by the first Event Rule whose Filter matches the Event, no other Event Rules will be applied. The system even records which Event Rule processed each event by storing a reference to it in the Event's **event_rule** field.

Each Event Rule is defined with an **Order** and a **Filter**. The **Order** specifies the order in which the **Filter** is going to be applied to incoming Events. An Event Rule with an Order of 50 will be applied before one with an Order of 100 (a lower Order takes precedence). These fields are extremely important for Event Rules because only **ONE** Event Rule can be applied to an incoming event.

Event Rules are applied right after Events are inserted into the **em_event** table. You will see that there is a slight delay, but it is only a couple of seconds.

Event Rules have just a few capabilities:

> **Create or update alerts.** The primary purpose of an Event Rule is to parse the data available in an Event (and ONLY the data available in that Event) to create an Alert. Event Rules have no scripting capabilities at all, and they cannot access any data other than the data provided in the Event. Before an Event Rule creates a new Alert, it will first check to see if there is an existing Alert with the same **message_key** value. If such an Alert already exists, then that Alert will be updated with information from the new event. If no such Alert exists, then a new Alert will be created with the value of the **message_key** field as specified in the Transform and Compose Alert Output tab of the Event Rule.

> **Compare against a threshold.** In an Event Rule, you can specify that an Alert is only to be created if more than X duplicate Events are received in time period Y, for example.

> **Bind to a CI.** The Event Rule engine, before creating a new Alert, will first attempt to find the most specific CI impacted by the Event under analysis. If enough data exists in the Event to find that CI, the CI will be **bound** to the Alert that's created. **Binding** a CI to an Alert means that the **sys_id** of the CI is stored in the **Configuration Item** field of the Alert. Having a CI bound to an Alert allows you to make smarter decisions when processing the Alert. NOTE: An Alert is bound to a CI; an Event is not bound to a CI.

Event Rules **have no scripting/programming capabilities.** This is because they need to be extremely fast and efficient. This is a critically important limitation. Alert Rules have almost infinite scripting capabilities through the use of Subflows and Actions. This means that if you need to make programmatic decisions with an Event, you need to first create an Alert from the Event (using an Event Rule), and then you need to look at using Alert Management Rules to apply your logic to the Alert.

20.3.2 Alert Management Rules

In contrast with Event Rules, multiple Alert Management Rules may be applied to a single Alert. When creating an Alert Management Rule, you define an Order and a Filter (with functions similar to those in Event Rules), and you also specify if the system should search for additional rules to apply, or if it should stop after this rule is applied. You can also specify if the rule will be applied to all Alerts that match the Filter criteria or only to Alerts that are updated such that they didn't previously match the Filter criteria, but now they do.

Alert Management Rules are evaluated by the system job named "Event Management – Evaluate Alert Management Rules", which runs every 11 seconds by default.

The most common purpose of Alert Management Rules is to create Incidents, but the capabilities are truly endless. While Event Rules can only create or update Alerts, Alert Management Rules can perform almost any action you can imagine. When you create an Alert Management Rule, you specify the Actions that the system will perform when the rule is applied to an Alert by specifying one or more Remediation Subflows to be called. A Subflow is a customizable set of steps that define actions to be performed, where each action optionally has components that can be customized via drag-and-drop (aka "a no code approach") or via script. It is the script customizations that provide you with the greatest flexibility.

As an example, the following diagram is a flow chart showing the application logic for the assignment of an Incident to a group.

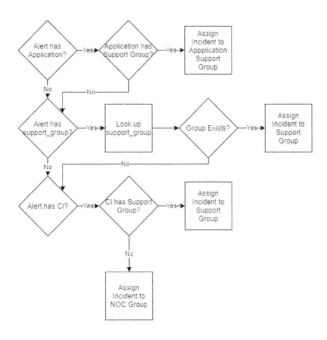

Figure 20-2 Example incident assignment logic

This logic can be implemented within a Subflow called by an Alert Management Rule. Your logic can be less complicated or can be exponentially more complex. The ServiceNow platform is powerful enough to allow as much customization as needed.

20.4 "Recommended" Event Rules Do not Do Much

Once you have events entering ServiceNow, the system will automatically try to identify patterns for events that do not match any Event Rules. You will see this message that allows you to view the recommendations:

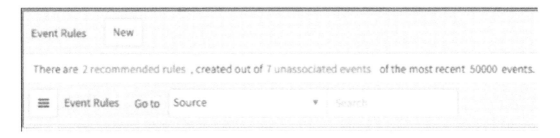

Figure 20-3 Recommended Event Rules

These Recommended Rules only identify patterns for event grouping and filtering. However, they do not customize much in the Transform and Compose Alert Output tab of the Event Rule (they parse the Description into some number of fields, but nothing is done with those fields, and the fields that are parsed may not be useful). Therefore, they do not do much to help you create Alerts. For example, if the affected CI is in the Description of an Event, these Recommended Rules will not parse that CI name, and they certainly will not put that CI name into a useful field of the Alert. Additionally, the Recommended Rules will usually build filter criteria that applies to one specific event on one host. That is not usually what you want in your Event Rules. There are some use cases for these Recommended Rules, but most of those use cases do not apply when you are migrating to ServiceNow Event Management from an existing event management system.

People unfamiliar with event management normally assume that these Recommended Rules provide some useful insight for Alert/Incident assignment or other important tasks, but they do not in the case of migration to ServiceNow ITOM. They do show you the events that have not matched any existing Event Rule filters, but you can get a similar list by searching the **em_event** table.

20.5 Alerts vs Incidents

A big question in most implementations is: When should an Incident be created vs just an Alert? The answer depends on your business requirements. To me, the big factor in this decision is the concept of SLAs (Service Level Agreements). An SLA in ServiceNow defines the response time requirements for responding to Tasks based on user-defined criteria. It also defines what actions and notifications are performed as the SLA timer counts down.

Without some extensive configuration and customization, an SLA cannot be attached to an Alert. The system is configured to allow an SLA to be attached to any **Task** record, like an Incident or Service Request. An Alert has fields like **Created On** and **Updated On** that can be leveraged to calculate how long it has been open, but that doesn't provide anywhere near the features of the SLA function within ServiceNow ITOM.

In my opinion, an Incident should be created for any Alert that needs to be monitored with an SLA. In most implementations, I have configured Alert Management Rules to automatically create an Incident for any Alert that has a severity of **Major** or worse (the easy condition). I usually create a separate Alert Management Rule to create Incidents for Alerts with lower severities that have been in an Open state for more than some amount of time. This gives teams time to handle the Alerts before an official Incident is created.

Through a process of Continuous Improvement, your organization will need to regularly review and discuss Alerts and Incidents in your environment. These reviews will lead to changes over time, and those changes will help you improve the responses to conditions in your environment.

21 Pull Connectors

One way to send events from an existing system to ServiceNow is through the use of a Pull Connector (listed under **Event Connectors (Pull)** in the navigator). A Pull Connector is a JavaScript (preferred) or Groovy (may be removed in the future) script that runs on a MID server to pull events into ServiceNow. Though Groovy may be removed in the future, I am mentioning it here because some of the existing connector scripts are written in Groovy, so you will need to be familiar with it if you plan to use one of these connectors. The following is the basic architecture of a pull connector.

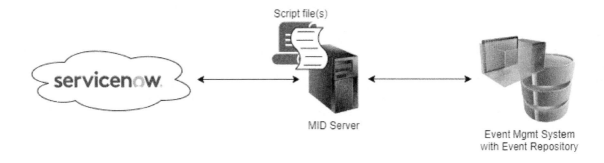

Figure 21-1 Pull connector architecture

21.1 The Required Pull Script

A pull connector must be defined to have at least one script, where that script will perform the pull operation. In this script is where all of the customization of the connector is performed. Some of the actions you will perform in this script are:

Defining a filter to pull only the appropriate events.
Setting the field values for the new events to be created in ServiceNow.
Possibly manipulating or parsing data in the events.
Logging messages for debugging.

The script itself is written in JavaScript or Groovy. You can really think of Groovy as Java in script form. The syntax is very similar to Java, but just a little different. If you are familiar with programming in general, you'll be able to work with Groovy with just a little help from Google. The MID Server (and the entire ServiceNow platform, actually) uses the Rhino JavaScript engine. That means that if you are familiar with JavaScript in the browser or in any other tool, you'll be right at home here.

The customizations you'll make to the script will be in the body of the **execute()** function.

21.2 The Optional Bi-Directional Script

If you want to update your event system with changes to Alerts that occur in ServiceNow, you will need to define your connector as bi-directional. The product documentation has a great example of how to do this, though it leaves out some details that I want to cover here.

21.2.1 Alert Field Identifier

When you select the **Bi-directional** checkbox in the connector definition, you then have the ability to specify the **Alert field identifier**.

Figure 21-2 Connector definition

The **Alert field identifier** is the field of the Alert that is sent to the connector script to uniquely identify the Alert for processing. Inside the connector script, you need to parse this value to find the appropriate field values you can use to identify the event to update in your existing event management system.

The documentation states that you cannot use any of the fields in the **additional_info** field as this identifier. However, as shown in the figure above, you **can** specify the entire **additional_info** field as the identifier. What this means is that for each Alert associated with this connector that was updated in ServiceNow, the entire value of its **additional_info** field will be passed to the connector as a string. Then in your connector script, you can convert that string into JSON and access any of the fields contained within it as appropriate.

Hopefully, you will find this piece of information useful. I used it at a client that was migrating away from an existing ticketing system. Because they were moving away from the existing ticketing system, they did not want to create custom fields in the **em_alert** table related to that system. However, they still wanted to update information in that system to keep in sync with the ServiceNow data. Using the **additional_info** field as the identifier field allowed the ticket number from the existing system to be passed into the ServiceNow Alert and back to the event management system for synchronization.

21.2.2 JavaScript

If your connector is implemented in JavaScript, then to enable bi-directional functionality, you need to first specify that the connector is bi-directional. You then need to add the **updateSource()** function to your script. The example script in the product documentation will give you all the guidance you need to do this. Basically, you just need to do the following in that function:

> Connect to the event management system
> Based on the data in the **Alert field identifier** that is passed into the function, update the event management system.

It is really very straightforward. The product documentation has an example of a custom bi-directional connector script you can find by searching online for **ServiceNow Create a custom pull bi-directional connector.**

21.2.3 Groovy

Groovy scripting appears to have been deprecated in ServiceNow, but there are still some legacy Groovy scripts in use. "Deprecated" essentially means that you can use the functionality, but you need to work to move away from it because the functionality will probably be removed in the future.

If your connector is implemented in Groovy, you have some additional work to do. Specifically, you're going to have to create a new JavaScript file that includes an implementation of the **updateSource()** function. The tricky part here is that you need to first create the script with the correct name in the **MID Server Script Includes**. You then need to specify the name of that script in the connector definition.

Figure 21-3 Groovy connector definition

For a Groovy connector, when you select the Bi-directional checkbox, the field named **Javascript to run** is displayed. This is where you provide the name of the "update" script to run. Yes, it seems strange that the pull connector is written in Groovy while the update portion is written in JavaScript. It is my belief that Groovy will be removed at some point in the future, so I would recommend against using it.

The name of the script you specify has to match part of the script itself. It must match the name of the variable storing the class created in the script. I have circled the matching text in the figure below.

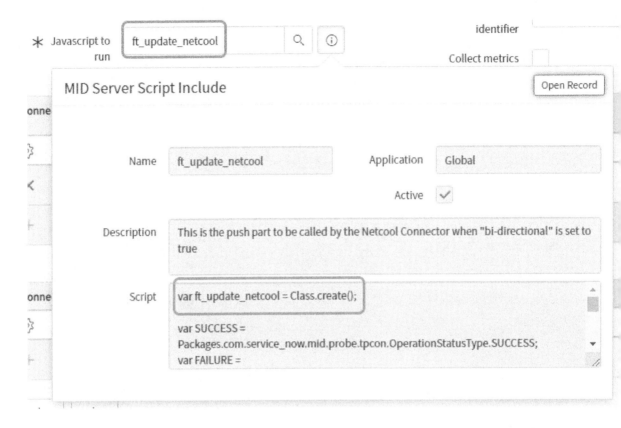

Figure 21-4 Script matches class name

If these names do not match, your script will not run, and you will see errors in the MID Server log files.

21.2.4 No Filtering

Any changes to Alerts that originated from a particular Pull Connector are placed on the queue for that connector when they are changed. The information placed on the queue is the **Alert Field Identifier**, its value, and the names and values of the fields that were changed. The bi-directional script does not have access to any other fields of the Alert, like **assignment_group** or **cmdb_ci**, for example. One limitation of this is the fact that you cannot filter out Alerts assigned to a particular group. Another example is that you cannot filter out Alerts that are bound to a particular CI. This normally is not a problem, but this behavior is important to note.

22 Alert Groups

Somewhat confusingly, this topic is separate from "Alert Grouping". ServiceNow Alert Grouping is a function that groups correlates related alerts to reduce the number of Incidents created. The topic covered here is about manually defining criteria by which multiple Alerts will be seen as a single Service.

An Alert Group, as defined under **Event Management->Services->Alert Queries**, is a Business Service that consists of a set of alerts that match a specified filter You create one by defining the criteria for your query.

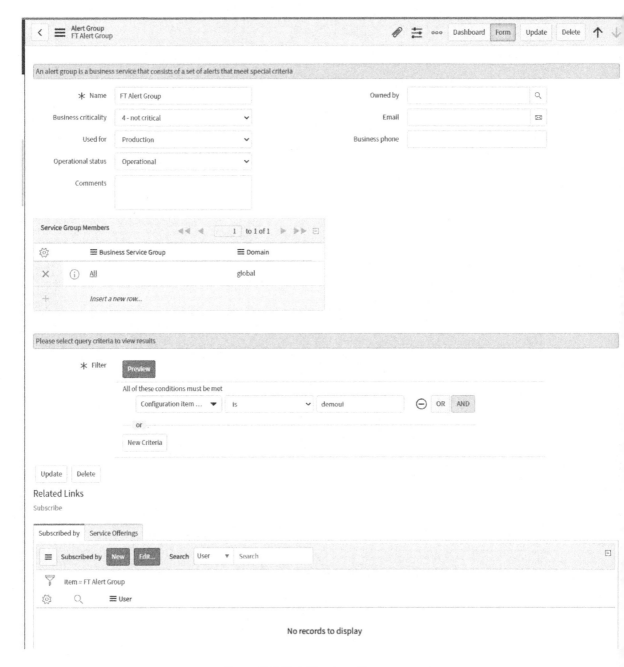

Figure 22-1 Alert Group creation

Once you create an Alert Group, you will see it in the Operator Workspace as a service.

Figure 22-2 Alert Group as a service

This is an easy way that you can create monitored services in your environment without reliance on the CMDB. It can be a very useful tool to help get your users into a service management mindset because you can group alerts based on criteria already familiar to your users. These groups can change or be deleted over time, but they help to group alerts into a meaningful context.

22.1 Alert Groups can completely define your Service Model

It is **possible** to leverage Alert Groups, along with the appropriate content in your Events, to create a Service Model that works perfectly for responding to issues in your environment. I think this is an extremely important point. If each of your Events contains information about the specific service(s) that are impacted, then you can use Alert Groups to group those Alerts into Services. The vast majority of my clients would see a tremendous increase in operational visibility (in a short amount of time, with very little effort) if they chose to take this route. Unfortunately, there is usually a steering committee of some sort that shoots down this "temporary workaround" in favor of attempting to fully populate a CMDB and associate each event with the lowest level CI possible. That is a valid goal for the (very) long term, but your users need robust and useful situational data that they can use to help resolve today's problems. Alert Groups are an easy way to give them that situational awareness.

23 ServiceNow Events Just Contain Data (no references)

The ServiceNow **em_event** table has ONE reference field, which is **alertid**. That's it. The ServiceNow way to make events meaningful/actionable is to associate them with alerts. Each event that comes into ServiceNow is a new row in the **em_event** table. Every. single. event. So if you're using a Pull Connector to pull events from your existing event management system, every time an event in your existing system is updated, that update will be sent to ServiceNow as a new event. Since this new ServiceNow event has the same **message_key** field value as an existing Alert, this new event will get associated with the same Alert that was created by the original event. The fields in the existing Alert will get updated with the new information contained in the most recent event.

From an ITIL perspective, each event needs to have some amount of operational information that allows it to be consumed and managed accordingly by the ServiceNow event management components. Part of your job is to ensure that events have enough operational information to be useful. For better or worse, there is no solid rule on exactly what this information is. At a minimum, the fields an event should contain are:

    node
    severity
    message_key
    description

Realistically, you should have some amount of additional data included also. You can provide as many name/value pairs as you need in an event. ServiceNow allows for this by defining the fields named **additional_info** as a String field that contains JSON data. JSON data is simply data in the formation:

{ name1: value1, name2: value2, ...}

Using this field should allow you to provide all necessary operational data in an event.

23.1 There is one exception

Each event **can** possibly contain a reference to a CI in the **cmdb_ci** field, but this is almost never the case. The only way the **cmdb_ci** field is populated is if an incoming event provides the **sys_id** for the affected CI. This is normally a step you might take at a later stage of maturity with the product. This is not something you're going to use initially.

24 CI Binding

An Alert is "bound" to a CI based on information in the initial Event that created the Alert. The following diagram depicts the flowchart of how an Alert is bound to a CI. The chart is a little different from the one you will find in the documentation, and I have provided a lot of details about each node.

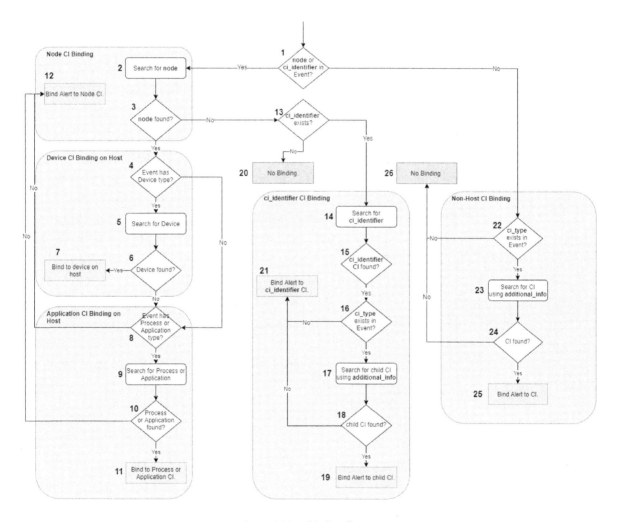

Figure 24-1 CI binding flow

There's really quite a lot of logic going on here, so I'm going to describe this flowchart with some details that aren't included in the product documentation.

1. An Event is created in the **em_event** table and is processed by the first applicable Event Rule whose filter matches the event. Event Rule filters are tested against incoming events based on the Order defined for the rule, starting at the rule with the lowest order. Remember, only ONE Event Management Rule can be triggered for any one event.

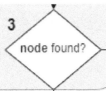

This decision node is asking the question: "Does the incoming event contain a non-empty value for either the **node** or **ci_identifier** fields"?

2. If the answer to **1** is Yes, then the system will search for a CI with a name, FQDN, MAC address or IP address that matches the value in the **node** field. The base class of the CI it's searching for is **cmdb_ci_hardware**. This means that it is looking for a CI that is an instance of the **cmdb_ci_hardware** class or any classes that extend this class. You can use the **CI Class Manager** to view the CMDB class hierarchy.

3.

3. Was a CI found based only on the value of the **node** field?

4.

4. If the answer to **3** is Yes, then check to see if the Event's **ci_type** field contains one of the following values: **cmdb_ci_file_system, cmdb_ci_network_adapter, cmdb_ci_storage_device, cmdb_ci_storage_volume**, These are the classes that the documentation refers to as "device classes".

5.	If the answer to **4** is Yes, then search for the appropriate device that exists on the host. This search is performed using the value of the **ci_type** and **additional_info** fields. As an example, let's say the **ci_type** field contains the value "cmdb_ci_db_db2_instance". Some of the fields defined for the **cmdb_ci_db_db2_instance** table are **db_name, running_process_command, po_number** and **name**. (The table contains other fields, but these are really the only ones that I think would be used to uniquely identify a CI of this type.) If **additional_info** contains any of these fields, then the values of those fields will be used to find the CI of this type. All of the field values need to match the values of the CI for the search to successfully match the Event to the CI. What this points out is that you need to be careful about the fields you pass in **additional_info**. If you're just adding fields to provide additional detail, I recommend using a custom prefix before the field name so that there's no collision with field names used for CI binding.

6.	Was a CI found based on the criteria described in **5**?

7.	If the answer to **6** is Yes, then bind the newly-created Alert to the device CI that exists on the host specified in the **node** field. To actually "bind" the CI simply means to store the **sys_id** of the appropriate CI in the **cmdb_ci** field of the newly-created alert.

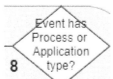

8.	If the answer to **6** is No, then check to see if the **ci_type** field value is any class that inherits from "cmdb_ci_appl" or "cmdb_running_process".

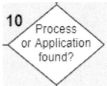

9.   If the answer to **8** is Yes, then search for the running process or application on the **node**.

10.   Is the running process or application found on the **node**?

11.   If the answer to **10** is Yes, then bind the new Alert to the CI. As stated above, this means to store the **sys_id** of the CI in the **cmdb_ci** field of the newly-created Alert.

12

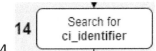

12.   If the answer to **10** is No, then bind the new Alert to the **node** CI.

13

13.   If the answer to **3** is No, then check to see if the Event has a **ci_identifier** field that contains a value.

14

14.   If the answer to **13** is Yes, then search for the CI based on the information in the **ci_identifier** field. This field value is actually a JSON string, so it contains data that looks like:
{ "name": "ORA_Instance1", "class": "cmdb_ci_db_ora_instance" }. One thing I want to point out here is that the fields in **ci_identifier** can be either the internal field name, like "sys_class_name" or the user-friendly display name, like "class". Additionally, the value for this particular field (**class/sys_class_name**) can either

be the internal class name, like "cmdb_ci_db_ora_instance" or the user-friendly display name, like "Oracle Instance".

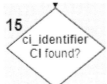

15.   Was a CI found matching all of the fields in **ci_identifier**?

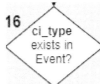

16.   If the answer to **15** is Yes, then check the event to see if it has a **ci_type** field.

17. ┌─────────────────┐
     │ Search for child CI │
     │using additional_info│
     └─────────────────┘
     If the answer to **16** is Yes, that means that we've found the "parent" CI, and now we're looking for the "child" CI. In other words, we're looking for a CI that has some type of containment relationship with the **ci_identifier** CI. Search for the child CI using **ci_type** and all of the appropriate fields in **additional_info**. As an example, let's say the **ci_type** field contains the value "cmdb_ci_db_db2_instance". Some of the fields defined for the **cmdb_ci_db_db2_instance** table are **db_name, running_process_command, po_number** and **name**. (The table contains other fields, but these are really the only ones that I think would be used to uniquely identify a CI of this type.) If **additional_info** contains any of these fields, then the values of those fields will be used to find the CI of this type. All of the field values need to match the values of the CI for the search to successfully match the Event to the CI. What this points out is that you need to be careful about the fields you pass in **additional_info**. If you're just adding fields to provide additional detail, I recommend using a custom prefix before the field name so that there's no collision with field names used for CI binding.

The **ci_type** field must contain the internal name of the class, like "cmdb_ci_file_system". It cannot contain the user-friendly display name of the class.

18.   Was the child CI found using **ci_type** and **additional_info**?

19 | Bind Alert to child CI.

19.   If the answer to 18 is Yes, then bind the Alert to the child CI.

20 | No Binding.

20.   If the answer to **13** is no, then the system cannot find a CI to bind to.

21 | Bind Alert to ci_identifier CI.

21.   If the answer to **16** or **18** is No, then the system will bind the Alert to the **ci_identifier** CI.

22 ci_type exists in Event?

22.   If the answer to **1** is No, then check to see if the Event has a value in its **ci_type** field.

23 Search for CI using additional_info

23.   If the answer to 22 is Yes, then search for the CI using **ci_type** and **additional_info**. As an example, let's say the **ci_type** field contains the value "cmdb_ci_db_db2_instance". Some of the fields defined for the **cmdb_ci_db_db2_instance** table are **db_name, running_process_command, po_number** and **name**. (The table contains other fields, but these are really the only ones that I think would be used to uniquely identify a CI of this type.) If **additional_info** contains any of these fields, then the values of those fields will be used to find the CI of this type. All of the field values need to match the values of the CI for the search to successfully match the Event to the CI. What this points out is that you need to be careful about the fields you pass in

additional_info. If you're just adding fields to provide additional detail, I recommend using a custom prefix before the field name so that there's no collision with field names used for CI binding.

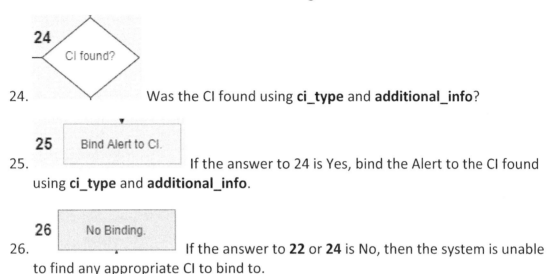

24. Was the CI found using **ci_type** and **additional_info**?

25. If the answer to 24 is Yes, bind the Alert to the CI found using **ci_type** and **additional_info**.

26. If the answer to **22** or **24** is No, then the system is unable to find any appropriate CI to bind to.

24.1 The bound CI may not have all of the information you need

The process of binding an alert to a CI is an important step in event management, and many ITIL practitioners want to use the CI as the sole source of Incident routing information. The reality is that there are normally several additional conditions that need to go into that decision.

For example, you might receive an event signifying a problem pinging a host. That host is the impacted CI for that event, and that host is owned and supported by an application group. However, you know from your knowledge of the environment that this type of event is almost always a network problem. In this case, you need some logic that considers the event itself to determine who needs to handle the issue.

Event rules alone cannot be used to implement this kind of requirement because they have a couple of limitations.

1. You do not have any scripting available to you in the binding process. Event rules are meant to be fast and efficient, and therefore do not have any scripting available within them. As a concrete example: the only way to implement an "if..then..else" block is with multiple Event Rules. A single event rule only has very basic logic: "If the filter matches an event, parse the event data as specified". Additionally, only ONE event rule will execute for any one event.

2. You only have data included in the event to help with the CI binding. There is no other data available within an Event Rule. You cannot access any tables or external data sources for more information from within an Event Rule.

The first place to add more complex logic is in a **subflow** invoked by an Alert Rule. A **subflow** is where you are going to implement the vast majority of your logic for Alert and Incident creation and update.

The way you actually perform work inside an Alert Management Rule is to call a **subflow.** (As of the Paris release, invoking **Remediation Workflows** from Alert Management Rules is deprecated, so I am just discussing **Remediation Subflows.**) The way to create an Incident is to call the **Create Task** action from within a **subflow** that is invoked by an Alert Management Rule. A built-in example of this is the **Create Incident** alert management rule, which calls the **Create Incident subflow**. (see figures below)

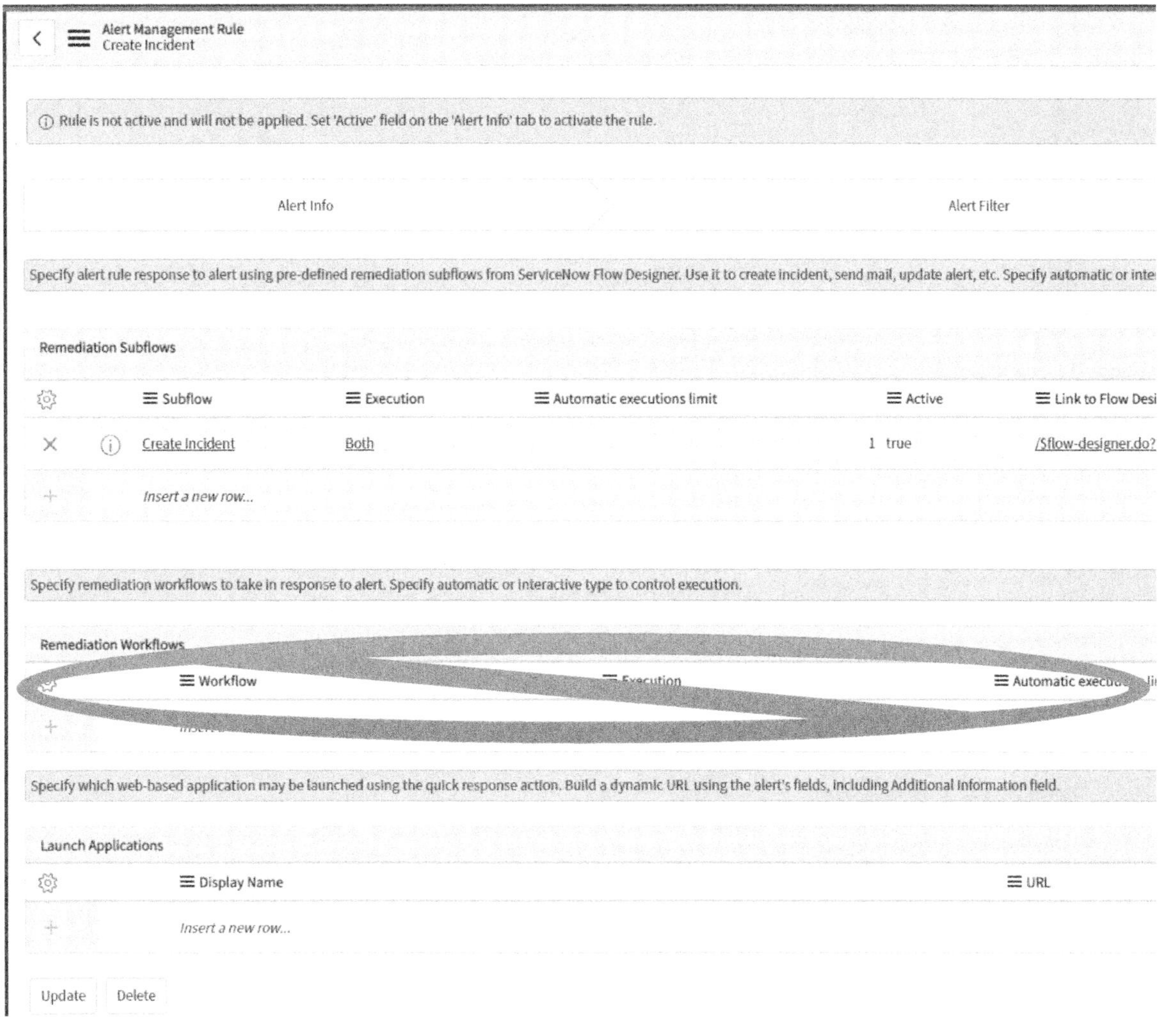

Figure 24-2 Create Incident Alert Management Rule

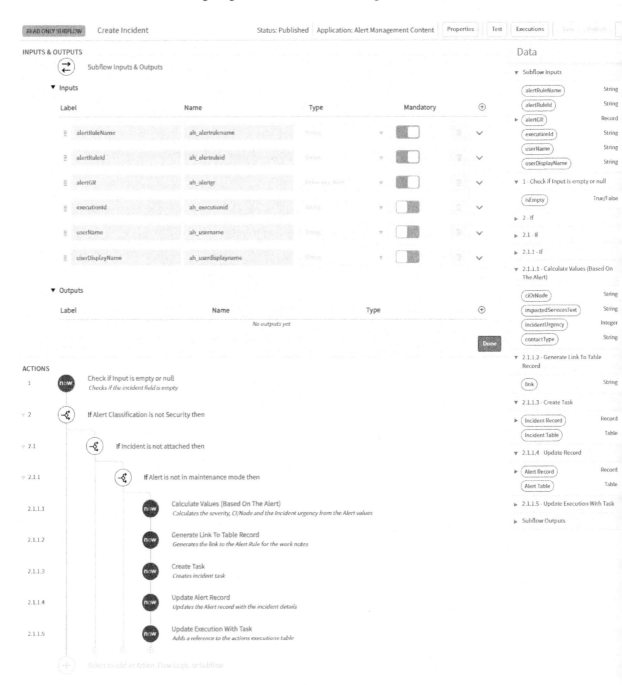

Figure 24-3 Create Incident subflow

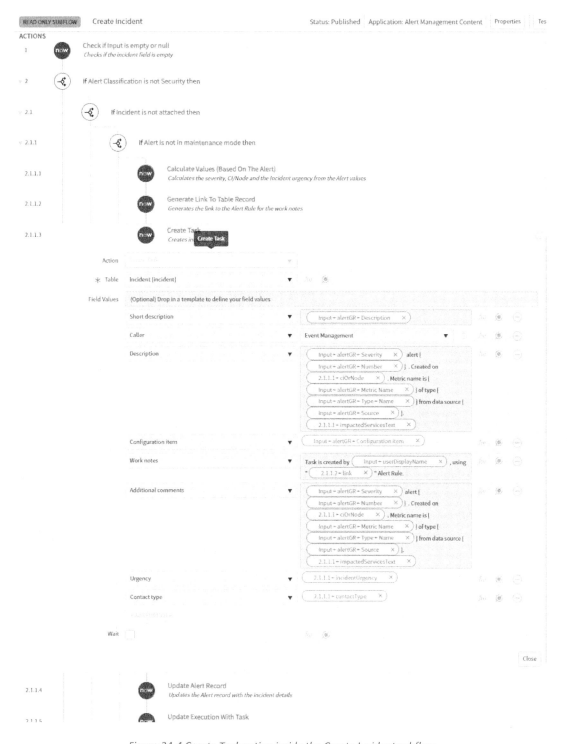

Figure 24-4 Create Task action inside the Create Incident subflow

The **Subflow Designer** is one of the low-code/no-code interfaces in the ServiceNow platform, and it is very powerful. As an implementer of Event Management, however, you're going to have to write some (probably a lot of) code. To do that, you're going to have to be very familiar with the scripting capabilities that are available in this interface.

The **Create Task** action is one of the many built-in actions provided in the ServiceNow Core. It is used to create a new **task**-type record in the database. This means that it can be used to create a record in any table that inherits from **task**, such as Incident, Problem, etc.

Normally, the CI for the Incident is the CI that is bound to the alert for which the incident is being created. But that is not an absolute requirement. You can actually specify any CI you want for an incident. This means that you can define a script for the Configuration Item field in the Create Task action where the script uses some kind of custom logic to find the correct CI for the incident. For example, the Alert may be bound to a particular server CI, but you can write custom logic to specify the Incident CI as a Business Application.

The main point here is that every field in an Incident can be populated via script. The default Create Incident Subflow sets the fields to values that should be correct, but you can copy that Subflow and change any of the field values you need to, such as Configuration Item or Assignment Group.

24.2 What does it mean to bind an Alert to a CI?

Binding an Alert to a CI at its most basic level means to store a reference to the impacted CI in the Alert's **cmdb_ci** field. The default Incident creation workflow will not create an Incident if the bound CI is in a maintenance window. Additionally, the bound CI is used as the primary search criteria for many of the impact analysis tools in the system. Your organization can reap many benefits from the product without binding Alerts to CIs, but binding each Alert to the appropriate CI unlocks a large number of additional capabilities.

24.3 Do I need to bind each Alert to a CI?

Technically, you do not need to bind each Alert to a CI. As stated above, ServiceNow ITOM is extremely valuable even if you do not bind each Alert to a CI. However, it is even more powerful if you do bind each Alert to the CI that is impacted by that Alert. Binding to the impacted CI gives you more searching, grouping, and prioritizing capabilities in the system.

25 Use A Separate Log Search Platform

Humio, Splunk, IBM Watson Discovery, Elasticsearch, DataDog, ServiceNow Loom or any of the competing products are built to store and search terabytes of data, while ServiceNow ITOM really is not, especially the **em_event** and **em_alert** tables. You want to keep these tables as small as possible while still allowing your users to see all the information that's required for their jobs. In practice, you should only keep Events from the last seven days (at most) in the **em_event** table and only keep open Alerts from the last 90 days or so in the **em_alert** table. By default, the **em_event** table is cleaned via the Table Rotation function built into the ServiceNow platform.

Alerts are automatically closed based on how long they have been inactive. This is done by a scheduled job named **Event Management – auto close alerts**. There is a separate auto flush process that deletes inactive records from the **em_alert** table. Details on auto flushes can be found under the **Table Cleanup** section in the ServiceNow navigator.

Before Event and Alert data is deleted, you should export this data using Web Services or Export Sets so that it can be stored in your log management system. This will allow you to view and historically report on older Events and Alerts. Many large organizations require that this data is kept for 18 months or more. If you are receiving millions of Events and creating tens of thousands of Alerts per day, trying to keep years of data will definitely impact performance on your ServiceNow instance.

While ServiceNow is a cloud-based PaaS application, it is actually just a traditional three-tiered application using a web server, multiple Java-based application servers, and a MariaDB database. Each instance is fault tolerant, highly available and extremely scalable, but it's not meant to run ad-hoc queries on millions of rows of data. That is where an external log search platform will shine for you. ServiceNow allows you to define custom UI actions that a user can take when viewing an Alert or Incident, where each one of these actions can launch an Alert- or Incident-specific URL. This means you can launch directly from the ServiceNow interface to any external application you want.

26 Ignoring Events

You can create Event Rules to ignore Events, which means that no Alerts are created for those ignored Events. This is perfectly acceptable for events that truly provide no value in your environment. Just realize that none of your ServiceNow operators will be reviewing the Events that you choose to ignore.

27 Custom Flow Actions

Once you have data in the alert **additional_info** field, you can easily parse that JSON data to pull out anything you need. One tool you can use to parse this data is custom flow Action objects. An Action can be invoked from a Subflow. An action accepts some number of inputs and returns some number of outputs. Those outputs can then be used in subsequent Subflow elements.

There are several Actions that are automatically installed with ITOM. One of these is **Calculate Values (Based On The Alert)**.

Figure 27-1 Screenshot: Calculate Values (Based On The Alert) action

You can see that an action has Input Variables, a Script body and Output Variables. In the Script body, you can write any custom logic you want. The primary purpose of this logic is normally to set values for the Output Variables, but it can actually be used to perform any functions you need in the ServiceNow platform.

27.1 Scriptable Field Values

Any action that has Input Variables allows you to provide a script to generate the values of those input variables. An example of this is the **Create Task** action that is included with ServiceNow ITOM. The following is a screenshot of the Create Task being called inside a Subflow.

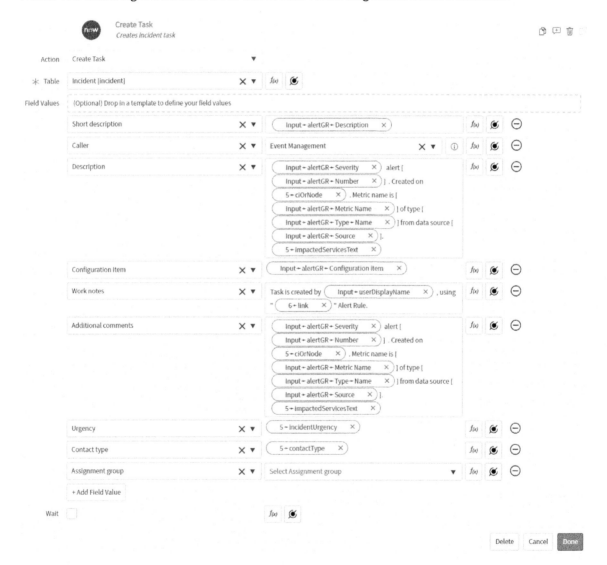

Figure 27-2 Create Task Action

To provide a script for a field value, you need to click the $f(x)$ button next to the appropriate field, which will display the script input section.

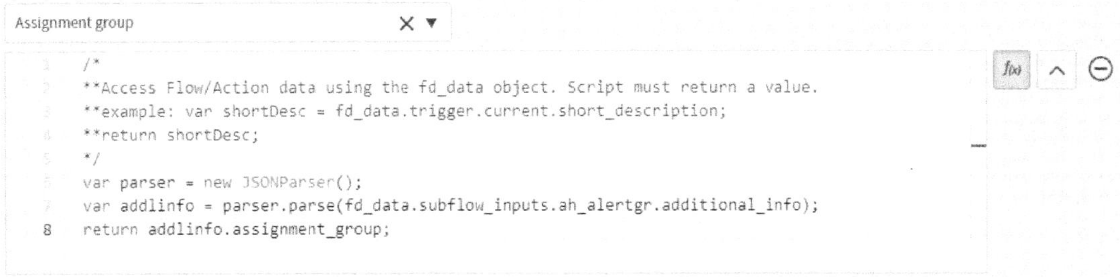

```
Assignment group                         X ▼

1   /*
2   **Access Flow/Action data using the fd_data object. Script must return a value.
3   **example: var shortDesc = fd_data.trigger.current.short_description;
4   **return shortDesc;
5   */
6   var parser = new JSONParser();
7   var addlinfo = parser.parse(fd_data.subflow_inputs.ah_alertgr.additional_info);
8   return addlinfo.assignment_group;
```

Figure 27-3 Field Values script input for Action

This example shows the code required to parse the **additional_info** field from the Alert into a JavaScript object so the individual name/value pairs are accessible using normal object.attribute syntax.

28 What About AIOPs?

You should leverage AIOPs (Artificial Intelligence Operations) as much as possible while still giving your users what they are expecting. AIOPs is based on learning patterns and actions over time. This means that on day one, no AIOPs implementation will know what to do with any particular event. AIOPs can recognize patterns, but your operations staff do not have the luxury of waiting for it to see patterns – your IT staff know that some things need to be done, and they need and expect to be notified about those.

ServiceNow ITOM includes an impressive AIOPs implementation, and you should leverage its capabilities wherever possible. The challenge is that any AI implementation needs to be taught or guided through its lifespan. Without training, you will have a mix of success, failure and confusion associated with the results of some of its actions.

The main AIOPs capabilities in ServiceNow ITOM are used for grouping Alerts and Incidents into meaningful context. However, the AI/ML (machine learning) functions do not do anything with Alert or Incident assignment. For that, you need to create custom logic to define the specific behavior that you want.

29 Work on Getting the Correct Information into Alerts

Whether or not your CMDB is populated yet, you need to get correct information into the alerts that are created so that they are meaningful and can bind to the correct CI. In most cases, the correct CI will not yet be in your CMDB, but that is a different problem. There are at least three approaches you can take here, and which one you choose depends on the direction that the stakeholders have agreed upon.

29.1 Store the "Eventually-Correct" CI Data in the Alert

In this approach, in the event rules, you will fill in the appropriate fields when creating the alert (**node**, **ci_type**, etc.) to bind to the CI that will eventually be in the CI. You then need to work with the appropriate groups to get those CIs created in the CMDB, preferably through discovery.

Pros:

You can easily see which Alerts are not bound to CIs, so you know which CIs need to be added.

You only need to do the event management work once.

Cons:

Your Alerts and Incidents will not always bind to a CI, which means they cannot be assigned correctly.

The CIs may never actually get into the CMDB, causing some amount of additional work to handle cases where the CIs do not exist.

29.2 Store Enough Data in the Alert to Allow Correct Assignment

In this approach, you will create Event Rules and customized Alert Management Rules to determine the assignment for Alerts and Incidents based on information included in the original event.

Pros:

Each event provides a combination of CI and assignment details that allow it to be processed as desired.

Cons:

You might lose some amount of governance over incident assignment by putting that decision into the hands of users.

29.3 A Combination of these Two

The **Case Study** at the end of the book provides details of an implementation using this strategy.

Pros:

Infinitely customizable.

Cons:

Can become complex. You may want to jump to the **Case Study** now to read about the solution implemented at "XYZ Corporation".

30 Compare Existing Tickets to ServiceNow Incidents

This is a tough task in most cases because you are changing your processes, so what constituted "a ticket" previously may not warrant the creation of an Incident in your new process. The purpose here is to show your existing users that every alarm that caused a ticket to be created in the previous system is still arriving in ServiceNow "somewhere". The goal is to ensure that users are still presented with the same amount of situational awareness in the new tool as compared to the old. This verification is essential for adoption of ServiceNow.

There are no shortcuts for this process. It involves creating a spreadsheet dump of your existing tickets and the Alerts and/or Incidents created in ServiceNow and then comparing the two lists to determine if anything significantly differs. For example, Alert Grouping may cause you to have fewer Incidents in ServiceNow when compared to the number of tickets in your legacy system. A decrease in the amount of "noise" is usually a goal of a ServiceNow ITOM implementation

31 Current Processes Need Organizational Exposure.

It is highly likely that the tools you have in place now are completely managed by individual teams, with no centralized data or governance. A huge challenge in many organizations is breaking this pattern. ServiceNow provides you with the opportunity to start to do things differently than they have been done before; basically, you can re-work processes to do them more correctly and efficiently now. This is an extremely frightening prospect to many teams because it changes large parts of what they do. Process improvement initiatives do not normally produce improvements at every step along the way. Usually, you have got to go backwards at several points to identify the correct behavior and then make the appropriate changes to facilitate that behavior. Again, education is a huge part of this process. The users need to be given all of the information they need to accurately envision the road ahead.

32 Event Table Details

resource vs **type**: use these to be as descriptive as necessary. The product documentation suggests vaguely that these two should be related, with resource being more specific than type. In reality, these are simply text fields that you can use however you like. By default these fields are used to create the **message_key** if you don't provide a value, but normally that will not be the case. It may make the most sense to have resource reflect the kind of resource being monitored, while type reflects the type of event. That may seem redundant or contradictory, but I will explain how they can be different. You may have a logfile monitor that generates events based on the messages in the logfile. These events may all be of the same kind ("LOGFILE_EVENT", for example), but they could be completely different. I am suggesting that you set your **resource** attribute to the kind of resource that is contained in the message that caused the event to be generated. And you could set the **type** to whatever process actually caused the message to be written to the logfile.

33 Testing server-side scripts

While implementing any ServiceNow product, you will have to write some number of scripts. With Event Management, most of those will be server-side scripts. The ServiceNow platform has a facility that allows you to test any script or to run ad-hoc functions via script. Navigate to **System Definition->Scripts – Background** to access this function.

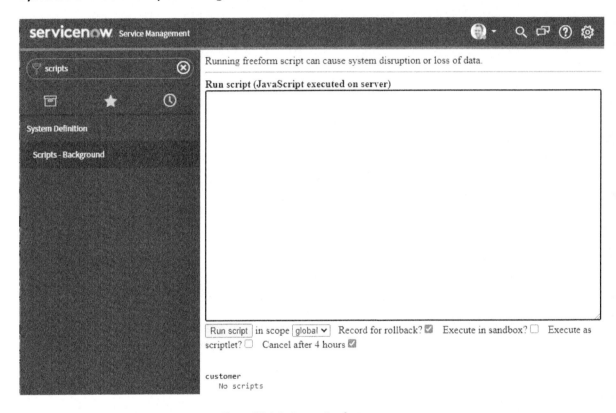

Figure 33-1 Script testing feature

Here you can type in any server-side script you want, keeping in mind that the script will be running on your instance and may impact performance. You normally will only use this facility in a TEST or DEV environment, but it's very handy.

Here is a screenshot of a sample script.

Figure 33-2 Sample script in tester

After clicking the **Run script** button, the following screen is shown.

Figure 33-3 Test script output

This screen shows the output written by the script using the **gs.info()** and **gs.error()** functions within the script.

34 REST API Explorer

The ServiceNow platform includes the REST API Explorer to make it easy to generate REST API Calls. Type **REST API Explorer** in the navigator to access this function.

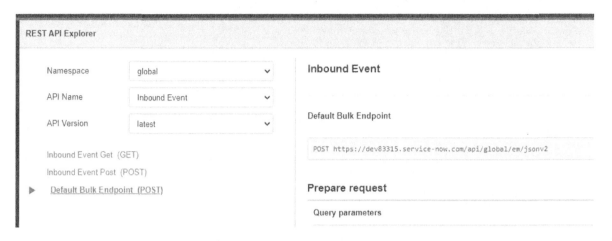

Figure 34-1 REST API Explorer

You can then use the product documentation to help you work through the parameters that need to be provided.

One great feature of this function is that it will generate the REST API call for you in one of seven different languages using the links at the bottom of the page:

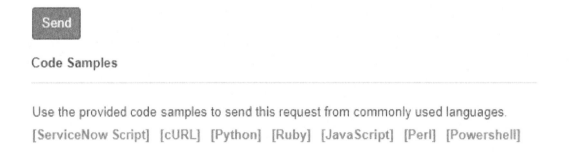

Figure 34-2 REST API Explorer Code Samples

Here is an example of a curl command that it can generate:

```
CURL Code Sample                                    Select Snippet      ✕

curl "https://▮▮▮▮▮▮▮.service-now.com/api/now/table/em_alert" \
--request POST \
--header "Accept:application/json" \
--header "Content-Type:application/json" \
--data "{\"acknowledged\":\"true\",\"classification\":\"product\"}" \
--user 'admin':'admin'
```

Figure 34-3 curl example

35 Customizing the Transform and Compose Form

The **em_event_rule_black_list** table is where you specify the fields to show in the Transform and Compose tab when creating or modifying an Event Rule.

Transform and Compose Alert Output

Compose Alert fields by adding free text and by dragging variables from the right pane.
Click Event Raw values to create **new regex expressions**.

Description	${description}
Node	
Type	${type}
Resource	${resource}
Message key	${message_key}
Severity	${severity}
Metric Name	${metric_name}
Source instance	${event_class}
Source	${source}
Classification	${classification}
Knowledge article	
Tags	${sys_tags}
Additional information	${AlarmName} , ${AlarmDescription} , ${AWSAccountId} , ${NewStateValue} , ${NewStateReason} , ${StateChangeTime} , ${Region} , ${OldStateValue} , ${Trigger} , ${LoadBalancerName} , ${region_id} , ${prefix} , ${punctuation1} , ${punctuation2} , ${object_id}

✓ Manual attributes

object_id	is	${LoadBalancerName}	⊖ ⊕

Figure 35-1 Transform and Compose Alert Output

In the screenshot above, you can see the field **Knowledge article** is displayed. That is because I've set **Show in rule** to **true** for the **kb** field in the **em_event_rule_black_list** table.

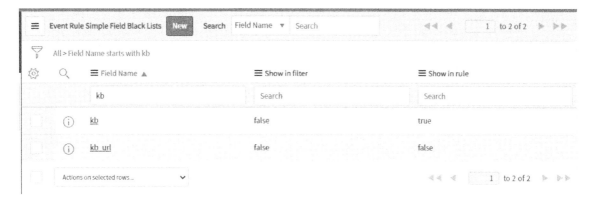

Figure 35-2 em_even_rule_black_list table

Section D: Case Study

This section provides some of the details of an implementation at one of my clients. The name "XYZ Corporation" is fictional, but the challenges and solutions presented are real. I have not included every change made, but I have tried to include as much detail as possible as it relates to the organization's migration from a legacy event management system to ServiceNow ITOM.

The chapters included in this section are:

I. Background

II. Organizational Information

III. Current Status and Capabilities

IV. Challenges

V. User Stories

VI. Core Issue

VII. Changed Event Content

VIII. Knowledge Base

IX. Event Rules

X. Alert Management Rule

XI. Action: Calculate Custom Values from Alert

XII. Subflow

I.   Background

XYZ Corporation has 15 year implementation of Netcool and a very old version of CA Service Desk for tickets.

No CMDB exists.

The Security team will not allow discovery to be performed without many months of testing and changes.

Events are sent to Netcool from a variety of different sources.

Each event has a field named **casdRoute** that contains a string. CA Service Desk uses this field, along with a support matrix to determine which group will be assigned a ticket.

All of the group names are being changed in the move from CA Service Desk to ServiceNow ITOM, so the values in **casdRoute** have no one-to-one mapping in ServiceNow.

Multiple groups are assigned tickets associated with the same device or resource.

II.   Organizational Information

a. Goals

Replace CA Service Desk completely with the ServiceNow platform. Keep Netcool in place for the known future. Any new monitoring tools that are introduced into the environment will be integrated directly into ServiceNow Event Management via the REST API. Netcool will eventually be phased out, but no timeline has been set for that.

III.   Current Status and Capabilities

All monitoring tools currently funnel through Netcool, which creates tickets in CA Service Desk. Only the event management team looks at the individual events that Netcool receives; the user community at large only sees tickets that are assigned to their group in CA Service Desk. Most of the tickets created in CA Service Desk are purely informational. (Moving to ServiceNow will be a large change because the users will be able to see all of the Netcool events (as ServiceNow Alerts). This will eventually provide invaluable additional situational awareness, but on Day One, this may induce a bit of information overload.)

All events are guaranteed to contain the following fields.

Netcool Event

alertGroup: contains the "type" of event. Each event type has a different format for the **summary** field.

casdRoute: contains the name of the "route group" in CA Service Desk.

casdRequired: 1 or 0 to specify if an incident should be created or not.

node: hostname of system affected by this event.

notifDest: List of email addresses that should be notified when this event is received.

notifRequired: 1 or 0 to specify if an email needs to be sent to recipients defined in notifDest.

severity: severity of event.

summary: a description of the problem that caused this event to be generated.

Figure III-1 Common Event Fields

This is a distillation of all of the background we were able to get

IV.   Challenges

They use IBM Workload Automation extensively for batch job processing, with over 15,000 jobs defined. The **cmdb_ci_batch_job** class exists, but has no relationships to any other classes, and there's no discovery tool for IBM Workload Automation.

There are a large number of events from log files. The only standard for these events is that they have values for **casdRoute**, **casdRequired**, **alertgroup**, and **summary**. The format of **summary** is different for each different event type. These are all user-defined, so they can really be anything.

There is no list of "known events" in the environment. The event archive contains 18 months of old events, so that is the data we used for analysis.

The Process Team initially decided that every Alert must be bound to the lowest-level CI affected. This was the primary directive for the first 12 months of the implementation, until the realization set in that the CMDB was missing most CIs, and that 99% of CIs had no administrative information. At that point, the directive was changed to "Try to route Alerts and Incidents to the correct group", which is the primary basis of this Case Study.

V.   User Stories

The following are the user stories that we extracted from users. During the time that these were collected, there was no common definition of a ServiceNow Alert vs Incident, so users gave us information based on their experience with CA Service Desk "tickets".

Tickets need to be assigned to the correct group and the appropriate people need to be notified.

- This one, seemingly simple requirement is almost the entire focus of this case study because it is the highest priority for all users of the system in the organization. The implementation could not be considered a success until this requirement was 100% met.

Each operator needs to view a list of tickets assigned to their group, including the location of the impacted host. This location is the primary piece of information used for triage.

Each engineer would like to see what applications are impacted by each ticket.

Management needs to apply an SLA to each ticket that has a severity of Major or Critical.

Management needs to apply an SLA to each ticket that impacts Application A.

Each application group wants to be notified when a problem occurs in one of their applications.

VI.   Core Issue

The crux of our problem was that there was initially a push to ONLY use CI information for the assignment of incidents, completely ignoring **casdRoute**. We fought for months to implement this directive but discovered that it was untenable. The largest hurdle was entering CI administrative data like Owner and Support Group. The original plan was to enter this information for all CIs (including individual processes and filesystems), but that was eventually seen as impossible (at least in the foreseeable future). Additionally, we found that individual CIs were supported by different groups under different circumstances.

The elegant part of the solution we developed was to use Knowledge Articles for two purposes:

1. as a mapping between **casdRoute** values and ServiceNow Assignment Groups;

2. and as a Known Error database containing runbook information.

Before users can send a new type of event into ServiceNow, they must make a New Event request from the Service Catalog. In that request, the user provides information that the system uses to correctly process the event.

VII.   Changed Event Content

For the existing events, we realized that we simply did not have enough information in each event to intelligently route it correctly if we ignored the **casdRoute** field. We needed to move away from using this field on new events, but there was simply no easy way to update all the existing event sources to change the existing events. To deal with the existing events, we created one Knowledge Article for each possible value in the **casdRoute** field. This will be explained fully a little later. For any new events created in the environments, we defined new fields that must be present. The following graphic describes the existing/legacy fields that are found in Netcool events, along with the new fields that will help routing in ServiceNow ITOM.

Netcool Event

alertGroup: contains the "type" of event. Each event type has a different format for the summary field.

casdRoute: contains the name of the "route group" in CA Service Desk. This is now mapped to a ServiceNow assignment group via a Knowledge Article with a similar value in its number field. DEPRECATED

casdRequired: 1 or 0 to specify if an incident should be created or not. DEPRECATED

node: hostname of system affected by this event.

notifDest: List of email addresses that should be notified when this event is received. DEPRECATED

notifRequired: 1 or 0 to specify if an email needs to be sent to recipients defined in notifDest. DEPRECATED

severity: severity of event. Values of 1, 2 or 3 automatically cause incidents to be created.

summary: a description of the problem that caused this event to be generated.

Existing

sn_ci_type: the internal class name of the affected CI (e.g. cmdb_ci_file_system)

sn_name: the name of the affected CI. Must match the name of the CI in the CMDB.

sn_kb_article: KB article number associated with this event.

xyz_application: name of the affected application. This must match the name of an Application Service that is defined in the CMDB.

xyz_assignment_group: the name of the group that that will be assigned any Alert or Incident created as a result of this event. This must match an existing Group as defined in the ServiceNow instance.

New

Figure VII-1 Event fields in Netcool

We did not change the structure of the Netcool ObjectServer database with these new fields. These fields only exist in the **EXTENDEDATTR** field of the Netcool ObjectServer. By default, this is a 4000-character field meant to store name-value pairs of data representing the original event message content plus any additional information desired. Here is a diagram showing the event message from the event source through a Netcool Probe to the Netcool ObjectServer.

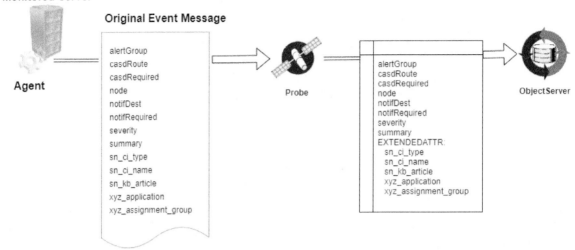

Figure VII-2 Event flow to ObjectServer

And here is a diagram showing the conversion performed by the ServiceNow Netcool Connector that we implemented.

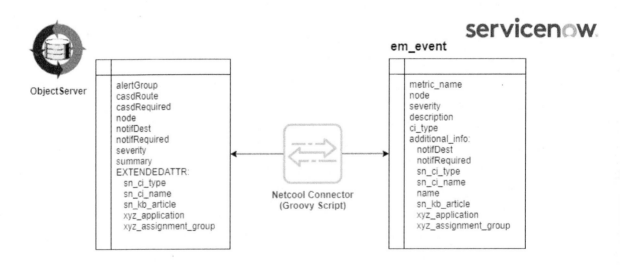

Figure VII-3 Netcool Connector conversion of event fields

Notice in the above diagram that our events have both a **ci_type** field and **additional_info.sn_ci_type**. The reason for this duplication is that needed to have the **ci_type** value in the Alert, but that field doesn't exist in the **em_alert** table. So we just kept **sn_ci_type** in **additional_info** so that the value would be available to our Alert Management Rules.

VIII.   Knowledge Base

To handle legacy events, for each **casdRoute** value, we created a Knowledge Article, with the **number** field equal to **KBCR<casdRoute_value>**. These knowledge articles in support of legacy events are just a temporary workaround because the mapping to assignment groups is not complete. Each Alert or Incident that references one of these knowledge articles is regularly reviewed to assess it for conversion to the new format.

We defined the new Monitoring Request process to be a request in the Service Catalog. Each new monitoring request that a user submits must include a new knowledge article. These Knowledge Articles act as a subset of the Known Error Database. Each event generated as a result of a monitoring request would contain a reference to the Knowledge Article in its **additional_info.kb_article** field.

We added several new fields to the **kb_knowledge** table so that we could use Knowledge Articles in our Event processing.

kb_knowledge

u_assignment_group: Reference to the assignment group that will be set for any Alert or Incident created in response to the reception of events that reference this article.

u_custom_script: Script field that is used when the processing of Alerts must be very customized.

u_incidentsev: Minimum severity of event that will cause an incident to be created.   **New**

u_emailsev: Minimum severity for emails to be sent out.

u_emaildist: Comma-separated list of email addresses to notify when an event with **severity >= u_emailsev** is received.

u_processing_directive: A numeric value to specify how Alerts are to be processed.

u_smssev: Minimum severity for SMS to be sent out.

u_smsdest: Comma-separated list of mobile phone numbers to receive SMS message when an event with **severity >= u_smssev** is received.

Figure VII-4 New fields in kb_knowledge table

IX. Event Rules

We created multiple event rules, with the goal of normalizing all of our events into Alerts with the exact same format. Because we had hundreds of different kinds of legacy events that we could not modify, we had hundreds of Event Rules in place. While that gets a little ugly, having this many Event Rules isn't a terrible situation. Each rule only has a filter and a transform, so it was straightforward to keep track of these.

X. Alert Management Rule

Only one Alert Management Rule was required because the logic is all in one Subflow. Using Event Rules to normalize all of the Events into properly formatted Alerts paid off for us because we only needed one primary Alert Management Rule to handle all Alerts, no matter which source they came from. We did have a couple of exceptional cases that required their own Alert Management Rules, but those were truly exceptional and there were very few of them.

XI. Action: Calculate Custom Values from Alert

This Action is what brings the whole solution together. Its logic determines how each Alert needs to be processed, and then performs that processing.

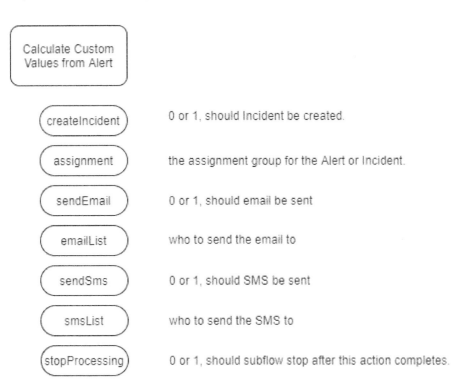

Figure XI-1 Output from action

Those variables are then available to the Subflow that calls the action. The logic diagram for this action is shown below.

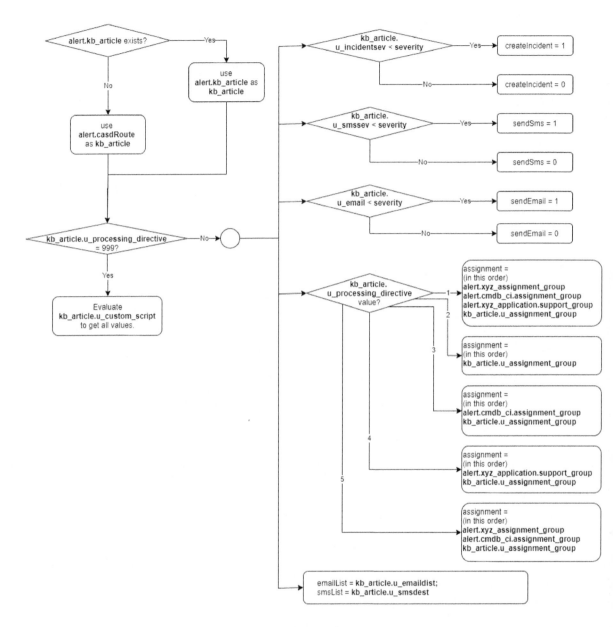

Figure XI-2 Logic diagram for action

This logic is implemented in the script body of the action. Most of the script is straightforward, but not the call to **kb_article.u_custom_script**. Calling this script is something like using the JavaScript **eval()** function, but it is safer because the creator of the script must have authorization in ServiceNow to update the Knowledge Article containing the script. Here is the code required to call the custom script and retrieve values from it.

This script is called from the **Calculate Custom Values from Alert** Action called in the main Subflow we defined. The following is the code used to call the script in this field:

```
gr = new GlideRecord('kb_knowledge');
// use the get(sys_id) function to get a specific record from a table when you know
// the sys_id of the record
the_article = gr.get(alertGR.kb_article.sys_id);
var evaluator = new GlideScopedEvaluator();
try {
   // pass the Alert GlideRecord variable to the script.
   evaluator.putVariable('alertGR',alertGR);
   evaluator.evaluateScript(gr, 'u_custom_script','');

   var routing_details = evaluator.getVariable('result');

   // the script invoked will set the 'result' variable to be an object with several
   // members:
   //
   // routing_details.assignment_group
   // routing_details.createIncident
   // routing_details.sendEmail
   // routing_details.emailList
   // routing_details.sendSms
   // routing_details.smsList
   // routing_details.errorstring
} catch (e) {
   gs.error('Error in evaluating script: ' + e);
};
```

As you can see, the script returns an object containing all the variables that need to be calculated by the **Calculate Custom Values from Alert** action, along with a variable named **errorstring**. This variable contains error information about any functions performed by the script that failed. This custom script can perform **any** operation in the system, so **errorstring** is used to return any errors from the calling Action.

XII. Subflow

Just one Subflow was defined for handling Alerts generated by Netcool events. The following is a screenshot of the actions taken by the Subflow.

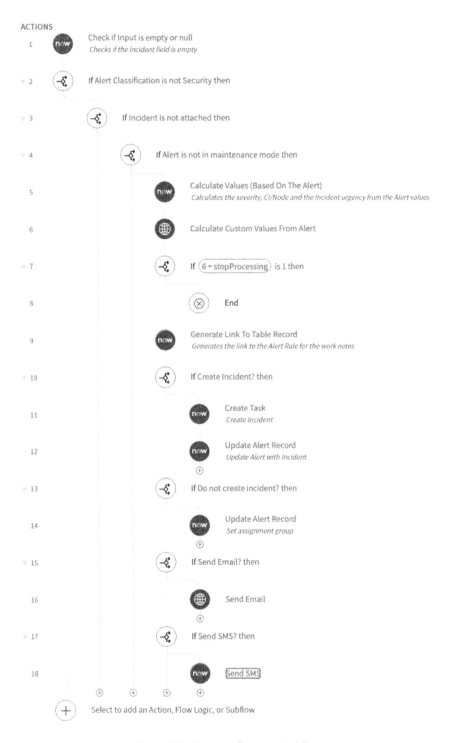

ACTIONS

1   Check if Input is empty or null
       Checks if the incident field is empty

2   If Alert Classification is not Security then

3   If Incident is not attached then

4   If Alert is not in maintenance mode then

5   Calculate Values (Based On The Alert)
       Calculates the severity, CI/Node and the Incident urgency from the Alert values

6   Calculate Custom Values From Alert

7   If (6 + stopProcessing) is 1 then

8   End

9   Generate Link To Table Record
       Generates the link to the Alert Rule for the work notes

10   If Create Incident? then

11   Create Task
       Create Incident

12   Update Alert Record
       Update Alert with Incident

13   If Do not create incident? then

14   Update Alert Record
       Set assignment group

15   If Send Email? then

16   Send Email

17   If Send SMS? then

18   Send SMS

Select to add an Action, Flow Logic, or Subflow

Figure XII-1 Actions of primary Subflow

The heavy lifting was done in the **Calculate Custom Values From Alert** action. This action implemented the flowchart shown in the previous section. As its name implies, it calculates values based on information in the Alert and the Knowledge Article. The bulk of that processing is used to determine who should be assigned the Alert and/or Incident and who should separately be notified. With all of those values calculated from the Alert and the appropriate Knowledge Article, each Alert could be handled appropriately.

Section E: Conclusion

I sincerely hope that this book has provided you with information and insight that you did not have before reading it. Whether you loved it or hated it, please let me know. You can email me at frank@franktate.com to send any comments or critiques.

The ServiceNow platform is an amazing framework that can help you to automate tons of processes and activities in your organization. Due to its capabilities and ease-of-use, I believe that it will be around for an exceptionally long time. My recommendation is that you should learn as much about it as possible through the product documentation, product training videos and third-party information available.

Good luck.

About the Author

Frank Tate is the founder and CEO of Gulfsoft Consulting, and has been working in IT Enterprise Systems Management for 30 years. His bachelor's is in Computer Science from The University of Texas, and he holds an MBA from LSU Shreveport. He also holds CISSP and PMP certifications. He has a passion for learning and for successfully integrating business needs with IT capabilities. He can be reached at frank@franktate.com, on LinkedIn (@gulfsoft) or on his blog: http://blog.gulfsoft.com.

Printed in Great Britain
by Amazon